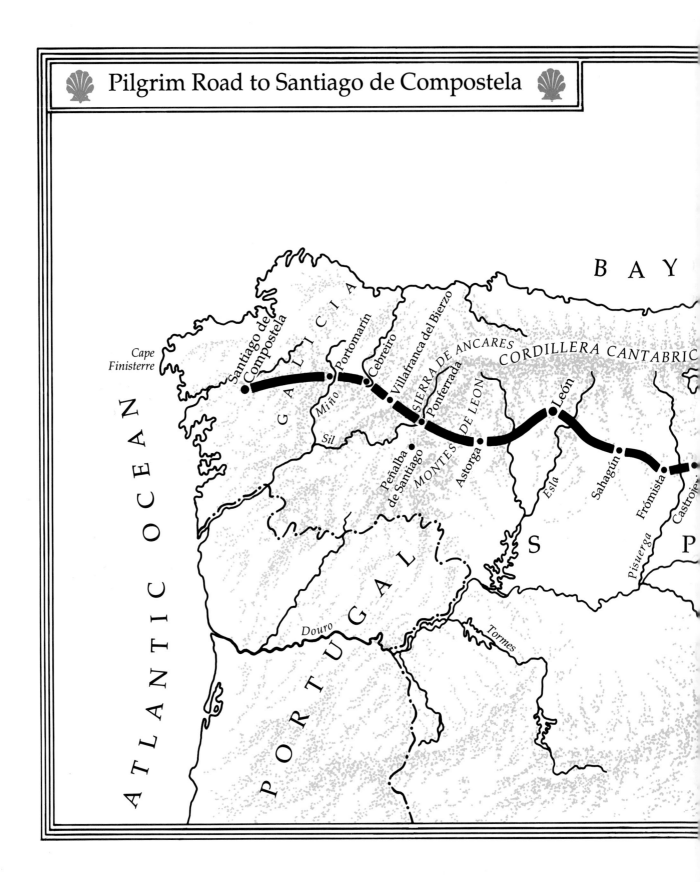

# Pilgrim Road to Santiago de Compostela

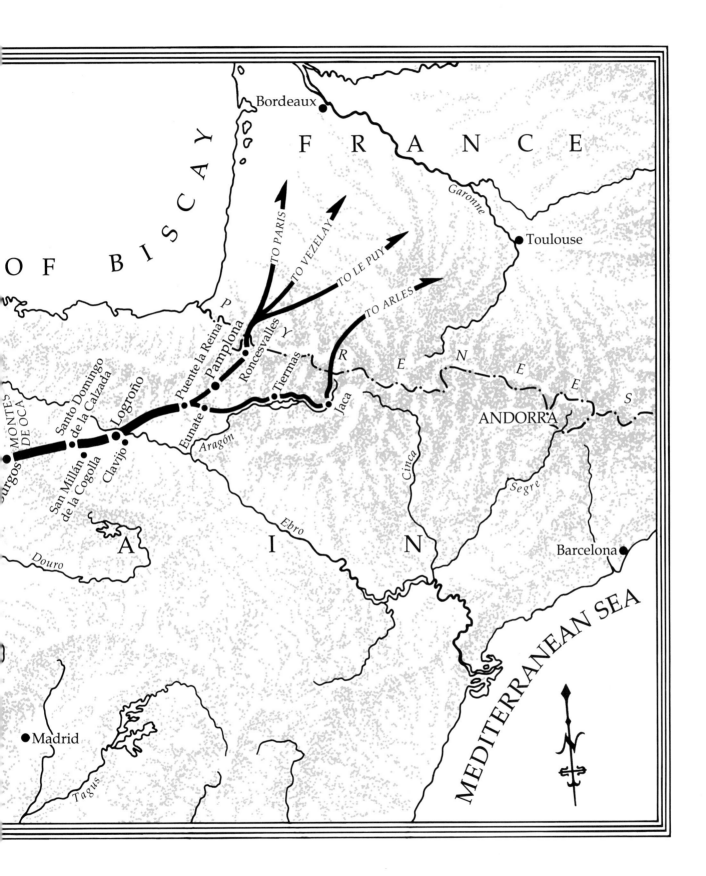

GULF OF BISCAY

FRANCE

Bordeaux

Toulouse

Garonne

TO PARIS

TO VEZELAY

TO LE PUY

TO ARLES

P

Y

R

E

N

E

E

S

ANDORRA

Pamplona

Roncesvalles

Puente la Reina

Tiermas

Jaca

Eunate

Aragón

Cinca

Segre

Santo Domingo
de la Calzada

Logroño

San Millán
de la Cogolla

Clavijo

MONTES
DE OCA

Burgos

A

I

N

Barcelona

Douro

Ebro

Madrid

Tagus

MEDITERRANEAN SEA

N

# SANTIAGO

## SAINT OF TWO WORLDS

*Photographs by Joan Myers*

ESSAYS BY
MARC SIMMONS, DONNA PIERCE,
AND JOAN MYERS

*UNIVERSITY OF NEW MEXICO PRESS*

Albuquerque

Library of Congress Cataloging in Publication Data
Myers, Joan, 1944–
Santiago : Saint of two worlds / photographs by Joan Myers ;
essays by Marc Simmons, Donna Pierce, and Joan Myers. — 1st ed.
        p.     cm.
Includes bibliographical references.
ISBN 0-8263-1273-X. — ISBN 0-8263-1274-8 (pbk.)
1. Santiago de Compostela (Spain)—Description.    2. Christian
pilgrims and pilgrimages—Spain—Santiago de Compostela.    3. Spain,
Northern—Description and travel.    4. Myers, Joan, 1944–    .
5. James, the Greater, Saint—Cult—Spain.    6. James, the Greater,
Saint—Cult—America.    7. James, the Greater, Saint—Influence.
8. James, the Greater, Saint—Art.    9. Civilization, Hispanic.
I. Simmons, Marc.    II. Pierce, Donna.    III. Title.
DP402.S23M94    1991
946'.11—dc20
91-6498
CIP

*Page i* The scallop shell and the red dagger cross are traditional symbols
of the Santiago pilgrimage. This key opens the door to the Church of St. James in
Villafranca del Bierzo, Spain.

# CONTENTS

# ACKNOWLEDGMENTS

One sunny afternoon, I stopped at a small shop selling religious objects near my home in Santa Fe, New Mexico. My companion claimed that his upcoming July 25 birthday was the "Feast Day of Santiago." Since neither of us had any idea who Santiago was, we decided to go in and inquire. That moment of idle curiosity followed by a succession of serendipitous co-incidences led to the several-year adventure of Old World pilgrimage and New World discovery that these photographs depict.

I am grateful for the early encouragement of Terence Pitts of the Center for Creative Photography in Tucson, Arizona; without his enthusiasm and his gift of a Spanish guidebook to the Camino, I doubt I would have seriously considered undertaking the project. Many people helped me in important ways over the three-year period that followed. I would like to give special thanks to Robin Gavin of the Museum of International Folk Art in Santa Fe, Marsha C. Bol of the Carnegie Museum of Natural History in Pittsburgh, Martha Egan, William Gruben, Annie Shaver-Crandell, Eleanor Munro, Marilyn Stokstad, Byron Johnson of the Albuquerque Museum, Lesli Allison, and John Menken. In Spain I am especially grateful to Don José Fernández of the Museo de los Caminos in the Palacio de Gaudi, José Ignacio Diaz, and Doreen Metzner of the Sociedad Estatal del Quinto Centenario. Funding for the Puerto Rico trip was provided by the

Albuquerque Museum. Gary DeWalt, David Douglas, and Michelle Zackheim offered needed criticism and helpful suggestions for my text. My collaborators, Marc Simmons and Donna Pierce, were a pleasure to work with. My editors, Dana Asbury and David Holtby, at University of New Mexico Press were supportive throughout the long process.

The journey is a powerful metaphor for our passage from life to death. The pilgrimage to Santiago de Compostela became a personal symbol for major changes in my own life. I would like to offer a special thanks to Reina Attias, Marcia Landau, and Michelle Zackheim who were always there for me on the darkest of roads.

*—Joan Myers*

# INTRODUCTION

The story of Spain and Spain in America has long been history's stepchild, at least for northern Europeans and North Americans. It is as if the Iberian epic in all its glory, tragedy, and raw turbulence somehow lay on the outer margins of significance—on the periphery of Western civilization's mainstream. But in today's world, which is tending to become homogenous, one finds it more and more difficult to ignore so substantial a subject as the Spanish contribution to the Western community.

The very geography of Anglo-America was a direct consequence of Spain's New World activity, since Englishmen moved to plant their settlements in areas the Spaniards neglected to colonize or passed by. Across the southern and southwestern present-day United States, from Florida through Texas and New Mexico to California, the Spanish crown created a row of buffer provinces to shield the silver-rich colonies below them. By the twists and turnings of fate, those same provinces in the nineteenth century fell under the glove of the United States, which thereby acquired a share in Spain's historical legacy.

British historian J. H. Plumb remarked in 1985 that "the United States has little sixteenth-century history," an observation that many unthinking Americans would probably accept as valid. But that century can only be dismissed as empty if one discounts the record of

Spanish exploration and attempted settlement, rejecting it as foreign to America's "authentic" national history. The unreasonableness of that position has been amply demonstrated by qualified writers who, summoning reliable historical evidence, have shown that one of the oldest and most persistent threads woven into the fabric of American life is our Hispanic heritage.

If that is truly the case, as it would appear, then it seems whatever illuminates the Spanish mind and world view also adds in some particle to an understanding of our national experience. With that point in mind, the authors of the present volume have approached the subject of Santiago (St. James), Spain's patron saint, in hopes of shedding light for English-speaking readers upon one limited but meaningful element in the equation that defines traditional Hispanic culture.

This book is divided into two parts. In the first part, I, as a historian and art historian Donna Pierce examine the peculiar phenomenon of Santiago, its origins and evolution through the Middle Ages to modern times. Our intent is neither to defend nor dispute the beliefs associated with the cult of Santiago, many of which in fact are highly implausible, but rather to convey some notion of the impact the saint produced upon Spanish history, religion, and art.

The second part presents a series of evocative images of the time-hallowed pilgrimage route across northern Spain to the ancient shrine of St. James. Photographer Joan Myers, who initiated the project that led to this book, tells in a highly personal essay how she was drawn to this work and what happened in the course of following in the footsteps of pilgrims. Out of her explorations, it becomes apparent, issued photographs that help us to see the connection between past and present and to grasp something of the richness and complexity of Santiago's legacy.

Readers should know that no new startling interpretations of Spain's great religious champion and patron are offered here. The authors, instead, have tried to pull together the main strands of the story as revealed by scholars, religious and secular, and to give a brief but comprehensive overview. In so doing, we have looked at the subject from several perspectives, in hopes of conveying an idea of the influence the tradition of St. James exerted upon Iberian civilization. It has been a challenging task.

—*Marc Simmons*

# SANTIAGO
*Saint of Two Worlds*

# SANTIAGO
## *REALITY AND MYTH*

### *Marc Simmons*

Finisterre the ancient Romans of Iberia called it: Land's End, or rather the End of the Earth. A jutting tongue of granite in the far northwestern corner of Spain, Cape Finisterre forms the westernmost rampart of the European continent. The heavy battlements of rock rising from the dark and storm-tossed Atlantic are often wreathed in thick mist. Sailors at sea catching a glimpse of the headland are moved to describe it as heavy, mysterious, haunting. Westward from the cape stretch two thousand miles of open water, which end finally on the beaches of the New World.

Immediately behind Finisterre sprawls the old province of Galicia, which occupies that portion of Spain north of the Portuguese border. Owing to its geographical position and configuration, Galicia might easily be termed the nation's panhandle. Rainy and cool, it is a land of brilliant green heights and rocky valleys whose lanes in summer are banked with a tangle of vines, grasses, and flowers. The Galicians speak their own language, which to foreign ears sounds closer to Portuguese than Castilian. From the stubborn landscape, they have had to struggle to wrest a living, so that even today other Spaniards regard them as poor, countryfied relations. Nevertheless, it was among the lowly Galicians, impoverished and without status, that the most enduring and significant legend of Spain had its origins in the Middle Ages.

According to the much-told tale, a hermit dwelled in an isolated vale of western Galicia, near the River Sar, about A.D. 813. His solitude was suddenly disturbed one night by the sound of angels singing. The voices directed his attention to a bright light, beamed from the sky, which illuminated a lonely spot thickly grown with woods and brush. The light seemed to radiate from a star, a familiar Biblical phenomenon that suggested to the pious hermit he ought to notify the local Christian bishop. Astonished by the report, Bishop Theodomir traveled from his residence at Padrón to investigate the matter. At his order, men cleared the site of trees and shrubs, and commenced an excavation. The earth soon yielded two graves, flanking a tiny chapel erected over a crypt. One version of the story says that the angels told the hermit in the beginning who would be found in the crypt, while another version claims that identity of the burial remained a mystery until the diggers revealed a name carved in the rough stone. In any case, when Bishop Teodomiro reverently pushed aside the lid of entombment, he was fully aware of what to expect. Inside, clothed and uncorrupted by the passage of eight hundred years lay the body of St. James the Apostle, known to Spaniards as Santiago.

To say merely that discovery of this grave was a landmark in Spanish history fails to do the event justice. For in truth, the finding marks the one preeminent moment in Spain's past which irreducibly charted the course of future events and determined the character of the nation and its people. Scholars innumerable, both native and foreign, have made that observation, so there is scarcely reason to doubt it. As the contemporary academic and philosopher Américo Castro explained it, the history of Iberia would not have taken the path it did without the belief that the body of Santiago reposed in Galicia. American author James A. Michener echoed that thought when he remarked that to understand the inner meaning of Spain, one must travel the road that leads to the grave and shrine of St. James.

But how did one of Christ's apostles come to be buried in the remote uplands of Galicia? And why would the presence of a crypt, even one as holy as this, produce such a profound impact upon a people's thinking? To answer these and similar questions is not a simple task, because from top to bottom the annals of Santiago are encrusted with unverifiable details, forming an account that is part history and part myth, with the latter unquestionably predominating. Indeed, Michener ventures to classify the whole thing as "a beautiful legend." Legend or not, the St. James story directly influenced some remarkable episodes in the histories of the Old World and the New, from the Pyrenees to the Strait of Gibraltar, and from New Mexico to the southern Andes.

The first order of business is to identify James and establish his connection with Spain. That furnishes the foundation for everything that follows. The best that can be said about his familial origins, sifted from conflicting claims made through the centuries, is that he was the son of the Galilee fisherman named Zebedee and his wife Salome, sister of the Virgin Mary. James's brother was the Apostle John, the two of them being favorites of Jesus who bestowed upon them the honorific surname of Boanerges, meaning "Sons of Thunder" (Mark 3:17). James and John, therefore, would appear to be the cousins of Christ.

Some of the early texts, both Christian and Arabic, however, refer to James as the brother of Christ, even on occasion as his twin brother. One source declares they were half-brothers, James being a son of Joseph by a previous marriage. For Spaniards, the notion of the brotherhood of Jesus and James has strong appeal since it lends immeasurable distinction to their national patron, Santiago. Américo Castro notes that while the belief that Jesus had a twin remained highly popular in Spain, it was declared heretical by the Church. And in any event, the mentions of James as Christ's brother, he adds, were meant in the spiritual or allegorical sense; that is, Jesus was a brother to all men.

The Spanish cult of Santiago, which evolved after the discovery of his crypt, Castro contends, displayed a mingling of Christian elements together with those left over from the early pagan religions of the Iberians and Romans. By way of example, he cites the curious parallel of the divine brothers Castor and Pollux, offspring of the Roman god Jupiter, known as The Thunderer. Thereby, they were designated "Sons of Thunder," foreshadowing Jesus's granting of that same title to James and John. In fact, this is but one instance illustrating how the titles and duties of pagan gods were transferred to the saints in the formative days of Christianity. The phenomenon remains well known to Catholic historians.

In ancient mythology, Castor, son of Jupiter, descended from heaven astride a shining white horse to become the protector of man and slay his enemies in battle. He was accompanied by his brother, also mounted on a white steed, who shortly returned heavenward while Castor stayed on earth to continue the struggle against foes of the faithful. The two were venerated in Roman Spain, and subsequently as Christianity replaced paganism, Santiago displaced Castor and emerged in popular folk belief as a sword-wielding equestrian saint who rode down from heaven in times of strife. This is simply to say that from remote antiquity, Spaniards were conditioned to believe in the supernatural figure of a soldier-horseman. Similarly, many of them associated Santiago with thunder, going so far as to credit him with causing it.

According to the Book of Acts, the disciples, following the Crucifixion, scattered to the far corners of the known world for the purpose of preaching the new religion. A persistent tradition, undocumented but not implausible, holds that James Boanerges chose, or was allotted, distant Spain as his missionary field. Sailing the length of the Mediterranean, he landed on the coast of Andalusia, about A.D. 38, and from there commenced a tour of the peninsula. His preaching of Christianity to the far-flung Spaniards consumed his energies for almost six years.

In the course of this evangelizing mission, James penetrated Spain's far northwestern corner, below Finisterre, where he found the rustic Galicians resistant to conversion. But, in neighboring regions he had more success, winning followers and founding three bishoprics. The last phase of his work took him across northern Spain to the ancient city of Zaragoza, below the Pyrenees. At that place occurred the miracle of the Pillar.

According to the tale, James initially won eight converts in Zaragoza. Nights, the small Christian congregation would assemble to pray at a secret spot near the Rio Ebro. Once at midnight, they heard angels singing, and suddenly the Virgin Mary appeared, standing on a marble pillar. Now, at that time, she was still a living woman in the Holy Land, so her visit to the Rio Ebro would probably be explained by the faithful as an example of bilocation—a miraculous phenomenon in which an individual appears to be physically present in two places at the same moment. The Virgin commanded James to behold the pillar, sent from heaven by Christ. She directed him to see to the building of a church upon the site, promising that God would perform miracles in it and that through her intercession Zaragoza would never lack for Christians.

James dutifully expressed his gratitude for bestowal of this sacred task upon him. Then, Mary gave him a holy image of the Virgin and Child, to stand in her place atop the marble column, and with that she had the angels whisk her back to Jerusalem. The apostle immediately began labor on the church, and he ordained one of his converts to carry it to conclusion and serve as priest. The edifice became the first church on earth to be dedicated to the Virgin Mary. A later replacement, the basilica of Nuestra Señora del Pilar (Our Lady of the Pillar), containing the revered column and image, can still be seen today.

Following this episode in Zaragoza, James ended his proselytizing and himself returned to Jerusalem. It was a misguided step. After briefly performing great miracles in the synagogues, he was arrested and beheaded by King Herod, thereby becoming the first of the apostles to suffer martyrdom. At the moment of his execution, tradition holds, an earthquake shook the ground and massive peals of thunder shook the heavens. If so, it proved a fitting tribute to one of the Sons of Thunder.

The body and head of the sainted James were tossed outside the city walls, to be devoured by dogs. But loyal Christians retrieved the remains, embalmed them, and arranged a temporary burial. Shortly thereafter, the body was disinterred and to the astonishment of all, the head was firmly reattached. After annointing the corpse with perfumes and sewing it in a deerskin bag, the devotees conveyed it to the port of Jaffa to be placed on a ship bound for Spain. In a voyage that lasted a mere seven days, according to conventional accounts, the vessel sailed past Gibraltar and up the west coast to the Galician port of Iria Flavia (later renamed Padrón). Of course, no ship of that era could have covered such immense distance in a week, so the chronicles consistently speak of St. James having been miraculously transported to his destination.

Just why it was deemed necessary to carry the body so far for burial remains part of the mystery of the entire affair. It has been suggested that St. James himself may have requested it before his death. Castro hypothesizes that Galicia offered a suitable gravesite simply because it was the farthest point in Christendom where the apostle had preached, near Land's End. At any rate, the two dedicated disciples accompanying the holy remains knew what they were about when they disembarked at Iris Flavia.

Promptly, they applied to the local pagan queen, named Lupa, for a parcel of land to bury their saint. But she referred them to a Roman official who tossed the two supplicant Christians into jail. An angel liberated them; other miracles followed, including the conversion of Queen Lupa; and finally a funeral party succeeded in transporting the body inland to a deserted cemetery where an abandoned crypt was pressed into service as a final resting place. Over the grave, members of the escort built a little chapel, and years later, when the two disciples died, their bodies were placed on either side of the saint.

At first local Christians cared for the apostle's tomb. Santo Iago they called him in Old Spanish, which eventually evolved to become the single word Santiago. In the course of centuries, however, the location and significance of the cemetery faded from memory, the chapel fell into ruin covering the crypt, and a bramble thicket obscured all traces. Not until almost eight centuries had passed, when the starlight alerted the hermit, did Bishop Theodomir come and rediscover the holy relics for all of Christendom.

King Alfonso II of nearby Asturias heard the news and hurried forward with several nobles of his court. On examining the crypt, he corroborated the astonishing discovery and forthwith proclaimed Santiago to be the official patron and celestial protector of Spain. The king, moreover, loosened his purse strings and paid for the building of a church and an adjacent monastery. Around these a town sprouted, afterward known as Santiago de Compostela, probably from the Spanish Campo de la Estrella, meaning "the field of the star." On being apprised of these events, Pope Leo III spread the news in a letter dispatched throughout the Church's realm.

From that point forward, Santiago de Compostela grew as a celebrated shrine and destination of pilgrims, ranking in importance alongside Jerusalem and Rome. The cult of Santiago flourished, and major historical consequences for Spain and for Christianity ensued. During the Middle Ages, for instance, it led to the crystallization of Spanish Catholicism and fueled the fires of Iberian nationalism. Fervid belief in Santiago, indeed, became a catalyst in the formation of the culture of modern Spain.

Not unexpectedly, authors and researchers both inside and outside the Church ultimately questioned the authenticity of the entire St. James narrative, from his alleged evangelizing mission, to the removal of his corpse to Galicia, and through the rediscovery of the lost crypt in the eighth century. No confirming document or record, contemporary with these events, is known to exist. Some of the first papers which refer to them in writing and date from the Middle Ages have been shown to be forgeries, or simply pure invention. Today, at the magnificent cathedral of Santiago, built in the eleventh century over the original gravesite, official guides carefully inform visitors that while St. James's story enjoys widespread acceptance among Spaniards, proof of its validity, based on historical fact, is lacking.

Over the centuries, devotion to the cult has proven indestructible. Believers dismiss the controversies stirred up by scholars and professional debunkers alike, and contend that faith based on the oral tradition is sufficient for their purposes and needs. Thoughtful writers acknowledge that the myth and its dimensions are less important than the fact that the cult produced fruitful politico-religious beliefs which had an impact on the reality of Spain's historical process. "The intensity of those beliefs," claims Américo Castro, "had immeasurable consequences." He adds: "The boundaries between the real and the imaginary vanish when what is imagined is incorporated into the very process of collective existence." British historian T. D. Kendrick seems to concur when he observes that "the Santiago creed . . . may be a dream, but it is a dream made real, and it is the dream that is the important fact in history."

Perhaps the key historical point to be made in that context is that the blossoming and prospering of the Santiago cult was dependent almost entirely upon a very real event in Spain's past—the invasion and conquest of the peninsula by the Islamic Moors, who first surged out of North Africa in A.D. 711, that is, more than a century prior to the finding of Santiago's crypt in Galicia. Within a year, the invaders had subdued most of Spain, leaving only pockets of resistance in the Cantabrian Mountains of the far north. Out of the happenstance of conquest, extraordinary events would flow.

At the start, Christian resistance to the Moors was feeble and disorganized. The Spaniards won their first small victory in 718 at Covadonga in eastern Asturias, a battle that later grew in the telling and assumed symbolic value. Notwithstanding, fortunes of the Christians remained at a low ebb for another century. Then came the stunning news of the unearthing of Santiago's remains and with it the prospect of an intensification of the war against the infidels. The anxiety of the times fortified faith in Santiago and gave hope to the Christian remnant battling the superior Moslem forces. Still, more centuries would elapse before the war attained the character of an all-consuming crusade.

In the meanwhile, according to the old histories, there transpired the truly marvelous battle of Clavijo, in the Ebro Valley, A.D. 844.

Out of it would be born one of the central themes in the Santiago legend. The Moslem princes from their capital at Córdoba had been in the habit of demanding and receiving one hundred Spanish virgins as an annual tribute. Ramiro I, king of Galicia, at length refused to comply with the infamous exaction and assembled an army, which numbered in its ranks an archbishop and five bishops, to face the Moorish legions that speedily marched against him. In their meeting at Clavijo, Rodrigo and his Christian partisans suffered a severe mauling and were driven from the field. In disarray, they fell back to cliffs at the edge of the valley and went into camp.

During the night, the king had a dream in which Santiago visited him. The apostle promised that the Christians would be victorious on the following day, their casualties minimal, and he himself, as protector of Spain, would participate in the battle. He even imparted instructions on strategy. At dawn, Rodrigo summoned his men. When he revealed his dream, they were fired with new zeal and courage. Returning to the field, abandoned the previous day, the enspirited Christian army hurled itself against the Moslem enemies. Sure enough, in the midst of the fray, just as he had promised, Santiago galloped out of the clouds on a pawing white stallion to lend assistance to the allies of the Lord.

Taking the lead, he swung a mighty sword and slew the warriors of Mohammed to the number of 60,000 or more. Evidently, many of his victims were decapitated. At least Church artists and sculptors have always thought so, for they consistently depict severed heads, turbanned and bloody, scattered at the feet of the raging steed. Santiago died in Jerusalem, beheaded by his foes, so perhaps it seemed just that he should mete out similar punishment, upon his miraculous reappearance on earth. Heartened by the sight of their patron saint knee-deep in blood, Ramiro's soldiers rushed in to complete the rout and claim the spoils. In so doing, they shouted the name of Santiago, using it for the first time as a battle cry. From then on the cry was voiced in every engagement with the Moors, and in time the Indians of the New World would hear it from the throats of the conquistadors.

After the battle of Clavijo, so the story goes, Santiago was definitively transformed into a militant and invincible saint, an image that was progressively magnified in spite of its obvious incongruity with the teachings of Christ. It was at this time, too, say many writers, that the apostle came to be called Santiago Matamoros, St. James the Moorslayer. Actually, that title did not come into use until the eleventh century, or about the time the first written mention of the Clavijo episode surfaces. Historians now seriously doubt that any battle by that name ever took place, nor was there any tribute of one hundred virgins. The whole thing was probably the imaginative invention of some Church scribe. Notwithstanding, popular belief holds that during the latter Middle Ages Santiago put in numerous appearances on the side of the Spaniards, and afterwards helped them in Africa and in both North and South America.

Soon after discovery of the apostle's body in the ninth century, pilgrims from Spain as well as all parts of western Europe began making their way to Santiago de Compostela, which in time rivaled Jerusalem in the number of its faithful visitors. Spaniards called the route leading there, the *Camino de Santiago,* or Road to Santiago. Mindful of the huge crowds that swarmed over it, they also referred to the Milky Way, with its myriad of stars, as the Camino de Santiago. English Catholics spoke of the Way of St. James, while continental Europeans identified the pilgrimage route as the Camino Francés, or French Road, since it wound through southern France before crossing the Pyrenees and heading westward toward Galicia.

From an early date, a scallop shell, worn around the neck or attached to the clothing, became the universal badge of the pilgrim. How that symbol originated depends upon which folk story one choses to believe. What is perhaps the oldest tale has it that St. James himself, while alive and preaching in Spain, baptized new converts using these shells. When riding out of the clouds at Clavijo, he was reported to have carried, in addition to his sword, a white banner emblazoned with a red cross and a scallop shell.

Another story credits the two disciples who brought the apostle's body to Galicia with introducing use of the shell. As they were landing on the coast, they beheld a runaway horse bearing a heavily armored knight into the ocean. The rider seemed certain to drown, but dozens of shells in a net of seaweed supported him until he could regain the shore. Taking this as a favorable omen, the Christian disciples selected the scallop shell as an emblem of their saint. In a different version, a mounted bridegroom was riding down the beach to his wedding when a giant wave swept him away and he drowned. The distraught bride appealed to Santiago, and forthwith the groom was restored from the sea, alive, his cloak covered with white shells.

The unceasing flow of pilgrims back and forth over the Camino de Santiago stirred up winds of change. They carried new European ideas into Spain, including influences of the French church and French styles of art and architecture. And they took back home knowledge of Spanish-Moorish culture and custom. An army of priests, merchants, innkeepers, artisans, and money-changers descended upon the pilgrimage route to profit from the traffic. And, to serve the masses of travelers, churches, monasteries, convents, inns, hospitals, and bridges arose in profusion. This veritable flood of pilgrims had the added effect of focusing attention upon the Moorish wars, thereby luring money and recruits in support of the Christian cause.

The church and shrine at Santiago de Compostela grew rich with pious gifts, while the chapels and monasteries strung along the pilgrimage road groaned under the weight of wealthy offerings. Moors marching up from the south raided the route with some frequency, having learned that booty was theirs for the taking. In the earliest years at least, defenses against these attacks were ineffectual.

Indeed, toward the end of the tenth century, a Moslem general from Córdoba proved unstoppable. Al-Mansur, a shrewd and cruel hunchback, proclaimed a *jehad*, or holy war, against the Christians. In 987 he ravaged Galicia. Approaching the walled city of Santiago de Compostela, he found it deserted. The inhabitants, as was their custom under such circumstances, had fled to mountainous precincts where

Moorish cavalry could not follow. Unopposed, Al-Mansur breeched the gates and sacked the city. So completely did he destroy the church of Santiago, that it was said not a trace remained. Only the tomb of the saint did he respect and leave untouched, along with an old monk who had stayed behind to watch over the relics of Spain's protector.

In demolishing the church of St. James, Al-Mansur salvaged the great bells and the heavy carved doors. Galician prisoners, taken in the campaign, were made to lug these things on their shoulders on the long road the Moors took back to Córdoba. There, in the central mosque of the Spanish capital of Islam, the doors were installed anew and the bells wrought into oil lamps. All of this was calculated to humiliate the Christians, while signaling their military defeat and the triumph of the Moslem religion. In fact, the affair was looked upon as a disaster without precedent in all of Christendom. More than two centuries would pass before it was avenged. In 1236 King Ferdinand of Castile and León would seize Córdoba and force captive Moors to haul the doors and recast bells back to Santiago again.

A characteristic of both Christianity and Islam was the emotional and religious significance attached to the physical remains, or even individual body parts, of leading figures. The Spaniards viewed the bones of Santiago as sacred relics, which thereupon assumed added status as a rallying point for soldiers committed to the destruction of the infidel. Some historians seem to think that before the cult of Santiago made its entry on the scene, the Moors already owned a powerful relic of their own, the actual arm of the Prophet Muhammad, secured within a vault in the Córdoba mosque. That arm inspired them in battle and contributed to the success of the original conquests. A contrary view, however, holds that an appendage of Muhammad was not heard of until sometime in the ninth century, and then it was a foot bone rather than an arm. According to this version, Moslem leaders recognized the power Santiago's relics conveyed to their enemies, so to compete they miraculously produced a piece of their own Prophet.

In any event, this situation is often cited to explain why Al-Mansur did not despoil the tomb and bones of Santiago when he had them within his power. His respect for the relics of holy men caused him to spare them. Perhaps a more likely explanation was offered by English travel writer Richard Ford in the 1830s who studied the matter and asserted that Al-Mansur never found Santiago's body, since Christians had hidden it before they fled. When later a new cathedral was built at the shrine, as replacement for the one razed by the Moors, the apostle's bones became so well hidden within that their location was completely lost. They were finally rediscovered in 1879, producing jubilant celebration, and today they rest in a wrought silver urn.

The Christian Spaniards and the Islamic Moors shared more than just a reverence for sacred relics. Among both peoples the making of a pilgrimage to holy places was a featured practice of the faithful. The example of the Christian pilgrimage to Jerusalem apparently prompted Muhammad to introduce a pilgrimage to Mecca as one of the precepts of his new creed. Santiago de Compostela and Córdoba became the focus of pilgrimages in the far west, just as Jerusalem and Mecca were the same in the eastern Mediterranean.

Another shared practice, the holy war or crusade, originated with the Moslems, but by the mid point of the Middle Ages had been borrowed by the Christians. In 1095 Pope Urban II proclaimed the first crusade to the Holy Land, but that was more than thirty years after the Spanish struggle against the Moors, the *Reconquista*, had been formally classified as a crusade by papal decree. The idea of a militant Christianity—soldiers of the cross aided by the saints—was, of course quite simply, a contradiction in terms. But in the context of the times and with the dramatic example of Islam, with its intermingling of religious and military motives, the new militancy assumed by the Church should scarcely surprise us.

The crusading zeal that burst forth in Spain and the rest of Europe during the eleventh century coincided with a revival of popular faith, papal reform, an expansion of the cult of saints, an enlarged devotion to pilgrimages, and a proliferation of ecclesiastical construction. As remarked, it was during this same period that many parts of the Santiago legend, the battle of Clavijo, for instance, first gained currency. The apostle's cult, therefore, became an integral component in the movement which merged Spanish Catholicism, military expansion, and the first stirrings of a dynamic nationalism. Indeed, the cult of St. James, carefully nurtured and fervently believed, is sometimes said to have made the Reconquest possible.

One indication of that can be seen in the increasing references to the intervention of Santiago on the Christian side during battles of the later Middle Ages. His presence uplifted Spanish spirits, inflamed their warlike passions, and granted divine sanction to their aggressive faith. His key role earned acknowledgment in an ancient paean which included this verse:

> *And when terrible wars had nigh wasted our force,*
> *All bright 'midst the battle we saw thee on horse,*
> *Fierce scattering the hosts, whom their fury proclaims*
> *To be warriors of Islam, victorious St. James.*

Another development of this period was the founding in 1170 of the military religious Order of Santiago. Like two other Spanish orders, Calatrava and Alcántara, it combined the ideals of monasticism and chivalry while pledging to defend Christendom against the infidels. Standard histories have long maintained that the chief duty of the Knights of Santiago was to keep the pilgrim road free of Moors and bandits. Virtually nothing exists in the documents, however, to confirm that such was the case. On the other hand, the Grand Master of the Order did sign an accord with the archbishop of Santiago de Compostela in which his men were declared to be "vassals and knights of the apostle St. James," and the archbishop, for his part, became an honorary member of the order, giving it a banner with Santiago's picture to be carried into battle.

All of the orders assumed a major role in the Reconquista, which progressively pushed the Christian boundary southward and confined the Moors to an ever diminishing territory. The Order of Santiago, not unexpectedly, emerged as the largest, most prestigious, and richest of these religious bodies. It defended the major frontier castles, ransomed Christian captives, administered cities and towns, ran hospitals and convents, and even sponsored a college in Salamanca. When called upon, the Grand Master could lead into the field an army of four hundred mounted knights and five thousand footmen, each one wearing a scallop shell. Once the last Moorish kingdom, Granada, was overthrown by Ferdinand and Isabella in 1492, the main purpose of the order dissolved. But it lived on, largely as an honorific organization, until all the orders were suppressed in 1813.

In the crucible of the long, bloody struggle with Islam, Spanish national character was forged. Among other things, the war had produced a hardening of the faith and an intolerance toward others, leading to the widespread notion that Spaniards were the new chosen people of God. The aid rendered by Santiago through the centuries, and the special relationship the nation enjoyed with him, seemed to confirm them in that conceit. As a result, pride and arrogance characterized the ruling classes of Spain, as well as the conquistadors who opened a new kind of crusade against the pagan inhabitants of the Americas.

One phenomenon of the Reconquista, in particular, was destined to have large consequences abroad—the marriage of interests and the close cooperation of the Spanish soldier and churchman. Crusades made them natural allies. Soldiers, at least those in military orders, took religious vows, while monks, abbots, priests, bishops, and archbishops joined armies and engaged in fighting. That curious custom and behavior was seemingly learned from the Moors. But it found its affirmation in and took as its model the image of Santiago, sword-wielding apostle who personified both the manly and religious ideal incorporated in the concept of *Hispanidad,* or Spanish selfhood.

The story of the Santiago cult furnishes a rich and vital thread running through centuries of Spanish history. It made its influence felt not only in the religion of the nation, but in its political and cultural life, economy, and military fortunes. The pilgrimage along the

Camino de Santiago reflected the spirit and living reality of Western Christianity, and as such it remains a phenomenon worthy of serious examination. James Michener perhaps phrased it best when he declared that the pilgrim's route to Santiago de Compostela remains to this day the finest journey in Spain, and one of the two or three best in the world.

When the Spaniards began to take ship for the New World in significant numbers at the opening of the sixteenth century, they carried with them the cult of Santiago as part of their cultural baggage. Not only was he the patron saint of the nation and empire, but he served as the special patron of all soldiers and horsemen. Invoking his name and bearing aloft his banner, Spanish explorers and colonizers would soon overspread major portions of two continents. Santiago marched at their side, they were convinced, and shared credit for many of the astounding triumphs chalked up by the sword and the cross.

His most visible and perhaps most enduring legacy throughout Latin America can be found in place names. Natural features such as rivers, bays, mountains, valleys, and plateaus were named for Santiago, as were cities and towns, together with plazas, churches, haciendas, and mines. In expanding geographical knowledge, the conquistadors saw to it that their special patron was well represented on the new maps they drew.

Fernando Cortés set sail on his earliest explorations from the port town of Santiago de Cuba, first capital of that Spanish island. One of his subordinates, Pedro de Alvarado, founded in 1524 the city of Santiago de los Caballeros, administrative seat of the Kingdom of Guatemala. From Santiago de Compostela, capital of the province of Nueva Galicia in western Mexico, Francisco Vásquez de Coronado set forth at the beginning of 1540 to explore the American Southwest. A year later, far to the south, the soldier Pedro de Valdivia named and laid the foundations of Santiago de Chile at the foot of the towering

Andes. Spaniards gave eighty-one settlements in New Spain (modern Mexico) the name Santiago. In Peru, the figure was twenty-three, and so on through the other kingdoms and provinces. These simple numbers merely reaffirm how closely the Spanish mind identified with the Apostle James and how eager was the colonist to honor him.

Nearly everywhere in America the expansion of Spain's boundaries and the imposition of colonial rule were attended by bloodshed. Indian resistance, from that of the advanced and populous Aztecs, Mayans, and Incas to the lowly Caribs and Chichimecas, crumbled before the armies of mounted and armored cavaliers who attacked with steel blades and bullets. Coming off their victory over the Moors at home, the Spaniards also enjoyed a strong psychological advantage. Had not their cross vanquished the crescent of Islam? Was not a New World immediately thereafter revealed to them, and with it were they not given a new, holy mission—to cross the Atlantic and spread Christianity to heathens, much like their own St. James had originally sailed the length of the Mediterranean to bring the Gospels' blessings to pagan Spaniards? As the chosen favorites of God, how could they fail?

These notions instilled a towering self-confidence and permitted the Spanish soldier to bear monumental hardships with equanimity and to face overwhelming numbers of Indian foes without flinching. They also encouraged him to view his battles with the native people as a continuation of the Reconquista. The early chronicles, for instance, drew curious parallels between the customs and behavior of Moors and Indians. Not unexpectedly, the apparition of Santiago on horseback, which had become the centerpiece in the folklore of the Spanish crusades, also embellished the histories of the Indian wars.

Some thirteen well-documented cases exist in which Santiago allegedly intervened in combat on behalf of the Spaniards. Four of the episodes took place in South America, the remainder in New Spain. The earliest occurred, 1518, in the swamps and jungles of Mexican Tabasco where the small invading force of Fernando Cortés experienced an attack by massed ranks of native warriors. At a perilous moment when the outcome seemed most in doubt, the beleaguered Spanish fighters saw confusion and disorder overtake the farthest columns of the Indian army, then spread through the entire body. The reason was suddenly revealed when they observed Santiago galloping out of the clouds to the rescue, and for good measure, riding at his side, the figure of St. Peter (San Pedro).

Both saints wore bright helmets and wielded swords that flashed in the sunlight. Santiago in the lead urged his warhorse over the fallen bodies of the infidels and within a short time forced the survivors to take flight. The Spanish knights eagerly joined the fray, uttering their spirited battle cry, *Santiago y a ellos!* ("St. James and at them!") Afterwards, they all gathered under a canopy and at Cortés's urging gave thanks to the Almighty for such a splendid victory. They compared notes, too, on the miraculous apparition of Santiago and San Pedro, the latter's unexpected presence being explained by the fact that he was the personal patron saint of Cortés.

Among the soldiers, the young Bernal Díaz del Castillo was the only one to say, in writing at least, that he had failed to glimpse the apparition. Long afterward when composing his recollections of the conquest of Mexico, he lamented: "It was not permitted to me, sinner that I am, to see either the one or the other of the Apostles on that occasion." Nor does he reveal whether he was witness to Santiago's return in 1520 upon the desperate flight of Cortés's army from the Aztec capital of Tenochtitlán (renamed Mexico City after the conquest). Now on a milk-white steed, the saint was reported by both Spaniards and Indians to have taken charge of the Christian squadrons. At his side this time, in place of Peter, was the Virgin, robed in white. She assisted him by throwing dust in the eyes of the infidel. Evidently, Bernal Díaz did finally catch sight of Santiago, later that year at the major battle of Otumba.

Of the other appearances of St. James, across New Spain, his presence in Nueva Galicia during the dark days of the Mixton War deserves special note. When the governor of the province, Vásquez de Coronado, marched away in 1540 to explore the northern interior, he had left his lieutenant-governor, Cristóbal de Oñate, in command of the government. Since the expedition had stripped the land of fighting men, oppressed Indians seized the opportunity and launched a bitter war against the newly formed Spanish towns.

Oñate mustered what forces he could and assailed the principal native stronghold on the heights of Mixton. Like crusaders at the walls of a Moorish castle, his soldiers charged the stony ramparts, but were repulsed and obliged to retreat in disarray to Guadalajara. Subsequently, a horde numbering 50,000 Indians laid siege to the Spanish community, burning outlying sections and gradually tightening the noose. Assembling the defenders, Oñate proclaimed, ¡Santiago sea con nosotros! ("May Santiago be with us!") and he led them in a fierce counterattack. The battle lasted three hours. Spanish losses were one man; Indian losses were reckoned at 15,000.

Within the ruined houses and outdoor ovens, the soldiers found numbers of the enemy huddled in terror. Upon interrogation, they disclosed that when one of the churches had burned a man on a white horse rode out of the flames. Dressed in a flowing cape, he carried a cross in his left hand and a sword in the right. Back of him marched an army of angels. This fearsome warrior had moved forward to join the Spaniards in their counterattack, an act that signaled doom for the Indians. Some of them had been struck mute by the spectacle, and others paralyzed. Indeed, the event seems to have left a lasting impression, as native communities of Nueva Galicia down through the centuries continued to commemorate annually this startling supernatural occurrence, which had proved, for them, a military disaster.

Sightings of Santiago continued through the colonial period and well into the nineteenth century. Oddly, during the wars for independence, the revolutionaries invoked the name of Spain's patron, calling upon him for assistance in defeating the loyalist forces of the king. One of Santiago's last appearances was recorded on February 27, 1862, when he joined the Mexican army in defeating a French force that had invaded Tabasco.

The influence of Spain's patron in the New World empire was further extended by the many aristocrats and high-ranking officials who held membership in the Order of Santiago. By one count there were 426 in colonial New Spain—viceroys, judges, treasury officers, governors, and generals. Conqueror Fernando Cortés was a knight of the order, as was Antonio de Mendoza, the first viceroy. Two sixteenth-century governors of the frontier province of Nueva Vizcaya, Diego de Ibarra and Rodrigo de Rio de Losa, were promoted to the rank of commander, a much-coveted honor within the Order of St. James. Such men of status encouraged veneration of the saint by the population at large.

The devotion colonial Spaniards showed to Santiago, and their summoning of his aid in battle is perfectly comprehensible given his role in the Spanish crusades of the Middle Ages. What appears puzzling was the rapidity with which the cult of St. James spread among the conquered Indians, for we would think their natural tendency would be to reject one of the most powerful symbols of their oppressors. But such, in fact, was not the case. Wherever Santiago was assigned as the patron of an Indian town, precinct, church, or mission, the people demonstrated an enthusiastic allegiance to his name and ceremonies.

When the conquest shattered the old Indian religions, Hispanic Catholicism moved quickly to fill the void. The natives, however, often managed to transfer the attributes and powers of their pagan deities to figures within Christianity. The Aztec goddess Tonantzin, for example, underwent metamorphosis to become Our Lady of Guadalupe, protector of Mexico and principal patroness of Latin America. Similarly, St. John the Baptist, associated with water, won wide popular acceptance in rural Mexico because of his identification with the native rain god Tlaloc. In a like manner, it was a consistent step on the part of the Indians to redirect homage for their traditional war god to the new warrior saint, Santiago. As victors, the conquistadors enjoyed enormous prestige among the native peoples, and not unexpectedly their favorite patron, St. James, had his reputation inflated by association with the new ruling lords of the land.

Popular ceremonies dedicated to Santiago spread to many Indian communities in Latin America at the very time that such celebrations were on the wane in Spain. With defeat of the Moors at the end of the fifteenth century, the Santiago cult had lost much of its momentum and intensity there. His feast day, July 25, remained a major observance, but one limited primarily, outside Galicia at least, to church services.

In America, the missionary orders gave no particular emphasis to Santiago, each one stressing rather its own favorite cults, as the Franciscans in New Spain, for instance, did with devotion to Mary and to the Blessed Trinity. It was the conquistadors more than the friars who kept attention focused on St. James, partly through their frequent practice of using Santiago as a place name. To cite an example, the Franciscans, in establishing the College of Santiago de Tlatelolco in 1536 to educate native youth, did not single out Spain's patron when they selected the institution's name, but rather, as a matter of convenience, they simply used the already existing name of the Indian barrio in Mexico City where it was located.

Wherever the name of St. James appeared, local festivals in his honor flourished, and the Indians assimilated assorted elements associated with his cult. In addition to the usual religious services conducted on the feast day, the native people celebrated with music, dance, fireworks, games, and horse races. Jockeys started a race by shouting in unison, ¡San-Tiago!, reminiscent perhaps of Spanish use of the name as a battle cry. An eighteenth-century writer observed that the Indians marked "the feast day of St. James with masques and dances in their own style to the accompaniment of a drum, oboes, and flutes out of tune and harsh."

Throughout much of Mexico can be found Santiago dancers, called *santiagueros*, who at the time of his feast participate in an outdoor ritual that is part dance and part folk drama. Wide variation exists in costuming and staging, as well as the dialogue. Men portraying Spanish soldiers wear picturesque suits and carry swords, or machetes. They speak and dance, and then fight turbaned Moors, forcing them to accept Christianity, which amounts to a symbolic reenactment of their own Indian forebears' defeat at the hands of the conquistadors. Much in the way of structure and style that goes into a santiaguero performance seems borrowed from the more formalized folk pageant brought from Spain, *Los Moros y Cristianos*.

As a feature of the native spectacle, the individual portraying Santiago customarily wears belted to the waist, front and back, a wooden horse that has been cut in two. Use of this "hobby horse," as it is sometimes referred to in the literature, is supposed to convey the impression that the dancer is mounted. In numerous Indian communities, the people believe the horse is endowed with life and venerate him. During the year, the keeper of the costume "feeds and waters" it daily. The same reverence is often extended to the santo, or statue, of St. James and his horse in the parish church. From the beginning, priests taught that such images were lifeless and powerless representations, but still the native folk persisted in worshiping them.

In the popular belief of the newly Christianized Indians, Santiago began to assume the role of their defender and helper. It was a mantle he donned easily, owing to his long and vigorous defense of the Church and the beleaguered Church membership. In Spain, the saint's attributes as warrior and national patron had overshadowed his less publicized role as protector of agriculture and ranching. But that was precisely the function of St. James that appealed most strongly to the great masses of rural Indians.

Throughout the villages and hamlets of New Spain, where churches were dedicated to Santiago, or at least an image was kept on a side altar, native farmers lit candles in his honor and offered prayers for protection of their crops and livestock. He was thought to be particularly effective in restoring strayed or stolen animals, and thus shepherds invoked his name frequently. Among the Tarahumara of northwest Mexico, for example, Santiago is said to have once made a journey through heaven dropping a trail of *pinole* (parched cornmeal) behind him so he wouldn't get lost. The pinole became the Milky Way, they believe, and the incident established Santiago's penchant for finding lost trails, including those of strayed stock.

The few customs and beliefs mentioned here represent only a small sampling from the large body of folklore that grew up around the name of Santiago in the New World. Just as the mythology of pagan Spain was drawn upon in the creation of the Christian cult of St. James, so too in his introduction to the peoples of America, there occurred an intermingling of aboriginal and European elements resulting in the emergence of an entirely new folk tradition. The congenial task of tracking the varied threads of that tradition is one that writers and scholars have only just begun to undertake.

⚜

In Spain, belief in the cult of Santiago had infused a population at war with spiritual energy and had served as a rallying point for the standard bearers of a newly emergent Hispanic nationality. Similar effects were produced in the overseas colonies, but there Santiago took on added importance as a symbol of Old World values which had to be defended in the face of New World threats. Among the galaxy of saints and many avocations of the Virgin, St. James remained a standout precisely because devotion to him lent an uncommon strength to peoples engaged in the dangerous and demanding task of pushing back frontiers. Brief reference to the ways the Santiago cult touched one realm within the Spanish Empire—the Kingdom of New Mexico, located in the present southwestern United States—can furnish a revealing case study of the saint's influence over a frontier population.

Less than a half century after Columbus's landing, Spaniards led by Vásquez de Coronado explored the *tierra adentro,* the remote interior country far north of Mexico City which was soon to be called New Mexico. The first of the native Pueblo Indians encountered by the expedition resisted, and as Coronado's chronicler Castañeda relates, "the Santiago was given and they were at once put to flight." The war cry of St. James would become all too familiar to those Indians in the years that followed.

Diarists of later expeditions remarked that the residents of New Mexico used bows like the Moors, some painted (tattooed?) their chins in the fashion of Moorish women, and the Pueblos worshipped in underground chambers described as mosques, but meaning, of course, the Indian ceremonial kivas. Such chance references demonstrate that the events of the Moorish wars remained fresh in the minds of colonial Spaniards, and in drawing a parallel between their own experiences and those of their crusading grandfathers, they would naturally persist in a firm devotion to Santiago.

Indian campaigner and wealthy silver magnate Don Juan de Oñate signed a contract with the Spanish Crown at the end of the sixteenth century allowing him to colonize the Kingdom of New Mexico. Leading the great wagon train of settlers which rumbled northward across desert and plains was a mounted page bearing aloft a banner of white Castilian silk. On it were emblazoned Oñate's coat-of-arms and a picture of Santiago astride his pawing charger. Afterward when a supply party followed the main expedition to New Mexico, it marched under a banner of red damask adorned with fringes of gold and silk and graced with the image of St. James and the Virgin. Most of Oñate's men wore polished armor, and as they rode behind the fluttering standard of Santiago there is every reason to believe they saw themselves as crusading knights, part of a warrior tradition that stretched far back into the Middle Ages.

When the Oñate caravan reached its destination in mid-August 1598—the Española Valley twenty miles north of the future city of Santa Fe—the colonists staged a celebration that included a bullfight, jousts, and the outdoor religious drama *Los Moros y Cristianos*. The similarity between their own situation and that of their embattled forefathers on the fields of Spain was brought home to them later in the year when disaster struck. Juan de Zaldívar, Oñate's nephew and second-in-command, had gone to Acoma pueblo to obtain supplies.

The Indian town was perched high atop a rocky mesa, and upon ascending the steep trail to the summit, Zaldívar and nine of his soldiers were set upon by the Acomas and slain.

Governor Oñate quickly sent Juan's younger brother, Vicente, with a force of seventy men to subdue the pueblo. At first view, Acoma seemed impervious to capture, so splendid were its natural defenses. But perhaps drawing upon strategy once used by crusaders to assail and take Moorish castles, Vicente de Zaldívar divided his slender army and ordered the main body to launch a frontal assault as a diversion. With the remainder, he scaled the rear of the mesa and managed to establish a foothold in one quarter of the pueblo.

The fighting raged with savage fury for three days. Then Acoma capitulated. The Indian survivors asked to be shown the outsized, noble Spaniard who had been in the forefront of the battle and had swept through their ranks like a whirlwind. He was astride a white steed, they said, and he had a flowing white beard, bald head, and carried a flaming sword in his right hand. This warrior was accompanied by a maiden of wondrous beauty. The Spanish men-of-arms looked at one another in astonishment. While having seen nothing of this, they knew instantly that Santiago and the Virgin had come to their assistance. So, they believed, the miraculous victory was explained: the seemingly impregnable citadel had been stormed and taken with the loss of but a single Spaniard.

From Oñate's day to this, Santiago has continued to occupy a conspicuous place in the religious life of Hispanic New Mexico. Many of the colonial governors proudly cited membership in the Military Order of Santiago as being among their most cherished honors. Presidial soldiers venerated Spain's patron, and the familiar image of the saint in which his horse tramples the severed heads of Moors forms the central panel in an eighteenth-century stone *reredo,* or altar screen, that originally decorated the military chapel on the Santa Fe plaza.

While no major church in New Mexico was dedicated to St. James, numerous small chapels were. Hand-carved statues representing Santiago, together with paintings on buffalo or elk hide, could be found everywhere. One of the most celebrated examples of such religious folk art is a small wood carving of a mounted Santiago, dating from the late colonial period and preserved in the Santuario de Chimayó, north of Santa Fe. That chapel is the destination of thousands of pilgrims annually during Holy Week. While their individual journeys are made in fulfillment of vows not specifically related to Santiago, nevertheless, the magnitude and intensity of the phenomenon are clearly reminiscent of the age-old pilgrimage across northern Spain to the tomb of St. James. Until recently, the parishoners of Chimayó even performed the ancient drama *Los Moros y Cristianos* outdoors on horseback upon Santiago's day, July 25.

Formerly, the feast of Santiago was commemorated in most New Mexican villages as a sort of Spanish national holiday. Indeed, the local people were in the habit of referring to July as *el mes de Santiago*, or the month of St. James. On July 25 nonreligious activities, following the customary church services, included games, horse races, cock fights, rooster pulls, and abundant revelry, the emphasis being on manly amusements as befitted a warrior saint. The custom also arose of serenading on this day persons whose given name was Santiago.

Not surprisingly, horsemanship played a prominent role in events associated with the celebration. Riders accompanied Santiago processions through the streets, ran races on the open roads, and pulled roosters. The *corrida de gallo*, or rooster pull, dates back to pre-Christian times in Spain. The unfortunate bird was tied by its legs and suspended from a rope stretched high in the air. Horsemen dashed underneath, rising in the stirrups in an effort to seize and wring off its head. More commonly in New Mexico, the rooster was buried to its neck in the sand. The *galleros* would gallop by and swinging from the saddle attempt to behead it. Often the whole bird was jerked from the sand instead, at which point the entire mob of horsemen pursued the man with the captive rooster, attempting to gain possession. In the process, the creature was torn to shreds.

The gory spectacle was laden with symbolism. Santiago, it will be recalled, had been executed by decapitation, spilling his blood as a Christian martyr. Participants in the *corrida de gallo* demonstrated their riding skills to please St. James, the patron of horsemen. They engaged in a mounted struggle and came away bespattered with rooster blood, marked as the caballeros might have been when they fought the Moors under the leadership of Santiago's apparition. The Pueblo Indians, who also engaged in rooster pulls on July 25—and still do—went so far as to liken the white, foamy lather that formed on their racing horses to the summer clouds which brought needed rain to their crops. Since in popular lore, Santiago was already linked to thunder, it required no great effort for the Pueblos to identify him symbolically as a bringer of showers.

As had the Indian tribes farther south in New Spain, the Pueblo people absorbed the figure of Santiago into native religion, reshaping him as an Indian deity with power to bestow supernatural blessing. Usually called Sandaro by the Pueblos (a corruption of "Santiago"), he appears as a dancer at public rituals. The Indian impersonator wears a Spanish-style hat and mask and carries a sword. About his waist, he wears an effigy horse, resembling the hobby horse seen in dances of southern Mexico, but larger. A cloth skirt, which forms the horse's body, reaches almost to the ground, concealing the man's legs, but not his moccasined feet. The Indians venerate the Sandaro figure by giving it prayer plumes and "feeding" it sacred cornmeal. This singular manifestation of St. James, so far removed from the standard European image, demonstrates the unexpected mutations that can occur in the evolution of specific elements of folk culture.

Santiago retained his strong appeal among New Mexicans as long as his special services were in demand. For instance, the last apparition of Santiago was recorded in the 1850s. A small group of settlers had moved into the San Luis Valley of southern Colorado and established a farming community. Daily the men traveled to distant fields leaving the women and children alone in their abode homes. One summer afternoon, the villagers gathered outside to await the return of their breadwinners and watch the build-up of storm clouds over the surrounding mountains.

All at once, they observed a large war party of Ute Indians thundering toward them. Knowing they were defenseless, the entire population fell to its knees, praying for deliverance. At the last moment, the painted warriors inexplicably turned aside, and the village was spared a massacre. The puzzling event was not explained until many years later, after the Utes had made peace. When questioned, the Indians admitted they had been riding to attack. But that intention had suddenly dissolved when they saw the figure of an armored knight on a white horse emerge from the dark clouds. None in the village had seen the apparition, but there was little doubt as to its identity.

By the last quarter of the nineteenth century, the danger from hostile Indians, which had plagued the Hispanic people for three hundred years, disappeared, and just as had happened in Spain following completion of the Reconquista, the fervency of devotion to Santiago declined. Nevertheless, he was far from abandoned, since he remained in the New Mexican mind an emblem of a persistent Hispanidad and a model of potent and knightly manhood. As New Mexico's Hispanic culture adapted to modern times, the image of St. James continued as a popular subject among native folk artists, and a scattering of public spectacles in his honor lingered on in out-of-the-way places. Santiago furnishes one of those visible links that still ties Spain to her lost children in the New World.

### SELECTED REFERENCES

A good introduction to the St. James legend, combining history and personal experience, can be found in the last chapter of James A. Michener, *Iberia* (New York, 1968). A more scholarly survey of the subject, one rich in detail, is the English writer T. D. Kendrick, *Saint James in Spain* (London, 1960). Readers should also find useful *The Bible in Spain* (London, 1906) by an English Protestant missionary, George Borrow, who went to Spain in 1833 and made some interesting observations about Santiago.

For the general background of Iberian history, against which the Santiago story evolved, two books can be singled out: Joseph F. O'Callaghan, *A History of Medieval Spain* (Ithaca, N.Y., 1975); and John A. Crow, *Spain, The Root and the Flower* (New York, 1963). Also, containing valuable references is William H. Prescott's old classic, *History of the Reign of Ferdinand and Isabella* (Philadelphia, 1837).

Among the many Spanish writers who have examined the Santiago phenomenon closely, Américo Castro has perhaps made the largest contribution. See especially his book in translation, *The Spaniards, An Introduction to Their History* (Berkeley, Calif., 1971). Recommended too is Emilio González-López, "The Myth of Saint James and Its Functional Reality," in José Rubia Barcia, ed., *Américo Castro and the Meaning of Spanish Civilization* (Berkeley, Calif., 1976).

Of several studies on the influence of St. James in the New World, the most complete is Rafael Heliodoro Valle's *Santiago en América* (Mexico, 1946). In his peerless narrative, *The True History of the Conquest of New Spain* (New York, 1966), the soldier Bernal Díaz del Castillo recounts several miraculous appearances by Santiago in battles with the Indians. For reference to customs and ceremonies associated with St. James in Mexico, see Frances Toor, *A Treasury of Mexican Folkways* (New York, 1947).

On Santiago among the Pueblo Indians of New Mexico, consult Elsie Clews Parsons, *Pueblo Indian Religion* (Chicago, 1939). Roland F. Dickey in *New Mexico Village Arts* (Albuquerque, 1949) demonstrates how Spanish colonists honored St. James. The miraculous appearance of Santiago at the battle of Acoma is described in Gaspar Pérez de Villagrá, *A History of New Mexico* (Los Angeles, 1933). What seems to be his last appearance in the Southwest, in southern Colorado, is told by Luther Bean, "The Miracle at San Acacio," *San Luís Valley Historian* 4, no. 4 (1972): 2.

# SANTIAGO

## *THROUGH THE CENTURIES IN ART*

## *Donna Pierce*

*"I would fain know why the Spaniards call upon that same St. James the Destroyer of Moors, just when they are going to give Battle, they cry 'Sant Iago, and close [ranks for] Spain,'" said Sancho Panza. . . .*

*"Thou must know, Sancho," answered Don Quixote, "that Heaven gave to Spain this mighty Knight of the Scarlet Cross for its Patron and Protector, especially in the desperate engagements which the Spaniards had with the Moors; and therefore they invoke him in all their battle encounters, as their Protector; and many times he has been personally seen cutting and slaying, overthrowing, trampling and destroying the Infidel squadrons; of which I could give thee many examples deduced from authentic Spanish histories."*[1]

The Santiago, or St. James, that Don Quixote and Sancho Panza were discussing began his road to fame as a fisherman in Galilee where he was called to the apostleship by Jesus Christ. Through the centuries his image was transformed by his own actions, medieval legends, miracles, and most important, through Christian belief. The site of his tomb became for a while the greatest pilgrimage center in Christendom, outside the Holy Land itself. This modest, though sometimes impetuous, apostle took up a sword in the Middle Ages and evolved into a symbol of the Church Militant inspiring the Reconquest of Spain from the Moors. St. James accompanied the Spanish conquistadors to the New World in their quest to subdue and convert the exotic peoples of the Americas. Three centuries later he helped Mexico win its independence from Spain. In art, St. James is depicted as either apostle, pilgrim, or warrior.

✠

## ST. JAMES AS APOSTLE

According to the New Testament, James and his younger brother, John, sons of Zebedee, were fishing in Galilee when they were called to the apostleship by Jesus. This scriptural reference to hired men manning their fishing boats implies that they were from a well-to-do family. James is referred to as James the Greater, meaning older or larger, to distinguish him from the other apostle, James of Alphaeus, or James the Lesser. John, his brother, is called John the Evangelist, owing to his role as author of one of the four Gospels, along with Matthew, Mark, and Luke. The brothers are believed to be cousins of Christ. As a result, James is often represented as physically similar to Jesus, with brown hair and beard, and John, who was younger, with brown hair and no beard.

In the Gospel of Mark (3:17) these two brothers were given the name Boanerges, which in the same verse is translated as "sons of thunder" and may refer to the impetuosity displayed by them toward an inhospitable Samaritan town (Luke 9:54). Along with Peter the brothers formed an inner circle of apostles who accompanied Christ in many of the important events recorded in the Gospels, such as the raising from the dead of the daughter of the ruler of the synagogue (Mark 5:37); the Transfiguration of Christ on Mount Tabor (Matthew 17:1); and the Agony of Christ in the Garden of Gethsemane the night before the Crucifixion (Matthew 26:37). On the Mount of Olives, Christ predicted his future resurrection to these same three trusted apostles, along with Andrew (Mark 13:3). James was the first of the apostles to die for Christianity when he was beheaded by Herod Agrippa before A.D. 44 (Acts 12:1–2).

Partly as a result of persecution during the Roman period, religious imagery among the early Christians was symbolic, rather than overtly Christian. In the catacombs, Jesus was depicted as a shepherd or as a lamb; his apostles, and other followers, as sheep. Examples can be seen in the early fourth-century frescoes in the catacomb of Saints Peter and Marcellinus in Rome and the mosaics in the mausoleum of Galla Placidia in Ravenna. This iconography was carried over into the mosaics of Christian churches in Italy such as San Prassede, Saints Cosmas and Damian, and Santa Maria in Trastevere. In the sixth-century apse mosaics of Sant' Apollinare in Classe near Ravenna, three sheep represent James, John, and Peter as they witness the Transfiguration. In one variation, the apostles appear as doves, such as in the baptistery at Albenga and Santa Maria Maggiore in Rome.

In the early Christian period, after the conversion of the Roman Emperor Constantine in A.D. 312, the apostles began to appear as twelve identical men flanking Christ and carrying sheep or scrolls. Examples from the fourth century survive in the Lateran Basilica and the catacomb of the Giordani in Rome. The apostles were sometimes identified by inscriptions bearing their individual names. According to tradition, the apostles gathered together before dispersing to preach the Gospel to all lands and composed the Apostle's Creed with each contributing one of the twelve propositions. St. James's contribution was the phrase: *Qui conceptus est de Spiritu Sancto, natus ex Maria Virgine* (Who is conceived of the Holy Spirit, born of the Virgin Mary). In artistic representations, the scroll held by each apostle often contained the phrase he contributed. This device serves the function of identifying the individual apostles. An example appears on the shrine of the Virgin at San Michele in Florence.

Aside from their roles as preachers, the apostles also serve as judges at the Final Judgment and, as a result, often appear flanking Christ in images of Christ in Glory, the Coronation of the Virgin, or the Apotheosis of a saint. Along with the prophets, the evangelists, and the angels, they make up the celestial court of Christ. This iconography is based on the scripture, "When the Son of Man shall come in his glory, ye also shall sit on twelve thrones, judging the twelve tribes of Israel" (Matthew 19:28; Luke 22:30). They fulfill this role in works as diverse as the mosaics of early Christian churches, the portals of medieval cathedrals (Plate 14), Raphael's *Disputa* in the Vatican, and the frescoes of Michelangelo in the Sistine Chapel.

Compositions of the twelve apostles progressively became less emblematic and more narrative. For example, they appeared grouped around Christ in a reenactment of the scene from Luke in which Christ instructs them to "Go ye, and teach the Gospel to all nations." Other examples based on the life of Christ—some scriptural, some apocryphal—depict the apostles in events such as the Delivery of the Keys to St. Peter, the Entry into Jerusalem, the Last Supper, and the Ascension of Christ.

Another theme that reflects their roles as preachers of the faith is the Descent of the Holy Ghost at Pentecost. The first important event after the Ascension of Christ and representing their task of spreading the Word without Him, the scene is based on the scriptural text, "And there appeared unto them cloven tongues, like as of fire, and sat upon each of them, and they were filled with the Holy Ghost, and began to speak with other tongues, as the spirit gave them utterance. . . . The multitude came together, and were confounded, because every man heard them speak in his own language." The ability to speak other languages was crucial to the success of their mission as preachers of the faith and is reflected in numerous works of art. A spectacular rendering appears in the principal dome of St. Mark's in Venice and another in the portal of the church of Sainte-Madeleine at Vézelay in France, both dating from the twelfth century. The word *they* in the scripture was apparently interpreted to include the women who attended the group, particularly the Virgin Mary and Mary Magdalen, and the women are often depicted in artistic representations of this event. The apostles, the Virgin Mary, and sometimes other women are usually grouped together with the Holy Ghost depicted in the form of a dove above them. Flames either descend from the beak of the dove onto the apostles and women or emanate from their heads. Representatives of the different cultures or language groups to be converted, all dressed in exotic attire, are often included. A related event depicted in art is the Dispersal of the Apostles. Armed with the ability to speak foreign languages, their individual field of mission was supposedly determined by casting lots.

Legend maintains that, upon the Dispersal of the Apostles, James remained in Jerusalem for a while. He then traveled through many countries before arriving in Spain, where he attempted to introduce Christianity. Initially James met with little success until one day, on the banks of the Ebro River, the Virgin appeared to him seated on a pillar of jasper and surrounded by a choir of angels. She instructed him to build a chapel for her on the site. He did as she instructed, and the church became known as that of Our Lady of the Pillar in Zaragosa where her image is still revered today. Thereafter, his missionizing crusade in Spain met with much success.

After his conversion of Spain, James returned to Judea to preach. There, according to legend, a sorcerer named Hermogenes set himself against James, just as Simon Magus did with St. Peter. Hermogenes sent his scholar, Philetus, to debate with James, but Philetus was quickly won over to Christianity. When Philetus returned to inform Hermogenes of his decision to follow James, the magician cast a spell on him that bound him by his hands and feet and then challenged James to free him. Notified of the spell, James gave his cloak to Philetus's servant to take to the scholar. As soon as Philetus touched the garment, he was freed from the spell. Undaunted, Hermogenes sent his demons to bind both James and Philetus, but James ordered them to do the same to Hermogenes. When Hermogenes's own demons brought him bound to James, the apostle freed him saying, "Christ hath commanded us to do good for evil." Hermogenes requested James's protection from his own demons. James gave him his pilgrim's staff for protection, and Hermogenes became his faithful disciple and preacher of Christianity.

Eventually, James was brought before the tribunal of Herod Agrippa. One of the Jews delivering James to the court was touched by his gentle demeanor, became converted, and requested to die with him. The apostle gave him the kiss of peace, saying "Pax vobis" (Peace be with you). They were both beheaded, but the kiss of peace has remained a ritual benediction in the church to the present. A sculpture of St. James as apostle holding a scroll with the words *Pax vobis* can be seen next to that of Christ on the tympanum of the south transept portal at the cathedral of Santiago de Compostela.

Since the Dispersal marks the last time the apostles were together as a group, later representations, of necessity, depict events in their individual lives. The most common of these are scenes of their respective martyrdoms, with St. James Major either being beheaded or already beheaded. As soon as the apostles began to be represented as individuals, each apostle was endowed with personal physical characteristics, such as white hair and beard for St. Peter, clean-shaven youthful looks for St. John, and dark hair and beard for St. James, a man in the prime of life. Such iconography can be seen in the mosaics of the baptistery of the Arians in Ravenna (fifth century) and Santa Maria in Dominica, Rome (ninth century).

In conscious association with the apostles, church architecture often incorporated twelve columns topped with relief busts of the apostles. Symbolizing the apostles' role in the foundation of the Church, twelve columns were used in the mausoleum of the Church of the Apostles in Rome and the Anastasis church in Jerusalem. Later, images of the twelve apostles adorned the columns or jambs of Romanesque and Gothic portals including those at Vézelay, Compostela, Chartres, and Strasbourg.

⚔

## ST. JAMES AS PILGRIM

From the sixth century on, the apostles were provided with distinguishing attributes. These were either symbols of their martyrdom, such as a sword for St. Paul and St. James, a cross for St. Andrew, and lances for Sts. Thomas, Thaddeus, and Matthias; or of their accomplishments, such as an eagle for St. John as evangelist, keys for St. Peter as head of the Church, and a pilgrim's staff for St. James in reference to his extensive travels. In his role as pilgrim, St. James came to be dressed with cloak, cape, and wide-brimmed hat, carrying a knapsack and staff topped by a water gourd (Plate 49). Eventually a scallop shell became associated with St. James and was added to either hat or cape.

After his martyrdom, the disciples of James retrieved his body but did not dare bury it locally for fear of desecration. Instead, they placed it aboard a ship, according to some versions, made of marble. Angels conducted the ship through the Pillars of Hercules (Straits of Gibraltar) to the northwestern coast of Spain, arriving in only seven days at the port of Iria Flavia (now Padrón) in Galicia. The disciples placed the body of the apostle on a great stone, which became like wax and closed around his body. This was taken as a sign that St. James wished to remain in Galicia.

Unhappy with this miracle, the ruler of the area, Queen Lupa, ordered that wild bulls be harnessed to the stone to drag it to destruction. When attached to the stone, however, the bulls became docile. Upon seeing this, Queen Lupa was immediately converted and built a magnificent church to house the sacred remains. St. James's two devoted disciples were eventually buried next to him.

In the period of confusion after the Moors invaded Spain in the early eighth century, the location of the body of the apostle was forgotten until around the year 813 when its whereabouts were revealed by miraculous vision to a religious hermit. In one legend, a field of mysterious lights attracted the attention of the hermit Pelayo who notified the Bishop Theodomir. The relics of St. James were found where the lights appeared. The name *Compostela*, Galician for "field of stars," may derive partially from this legend.

After the rediscovery of the tomb of St. James, King Alfonso II of Asturias (792–842) built a church over the tomb, and it became a pilgrimage center. When Iria was sacked by Norsemen (c. 850), the bishopric was moved to nearby Compostela, and Alfonso III (866–

911) built a larger church. Consecrated in 899, this later church became a national shrine for the new kingdom of León and kings were crowned there. In 997 the Moorish caliphate Al-Mansur of Córdoba destroyed Compostela but did not damage the tomb. A new church was consecrated in 1003. The existing church was begun in 1075.

"New when Spain was new in the early days of the Reconquest, greatest in the Age of Faith, made richer and poorer like so much else by the Renaissance, it comes to us eleven centuries old, but with its spiritual quality still young and fresh, sweet with the unquenchable beauty that characterizes all things for which the Middle Ages really cared."[2] So said art historian Kenneth John Conant in the early twentieth century when discussing the pilgrimage to Santiago in his great study of the cathedral.

News of the discovery of the relics spread quickly, and pilgrimages to Compostela began early. By the mid-900s both civil and ecclesiastical dignitaries from all over Europe were making the journey to Compostela. By the twelfth century even royalty and holy persons were coming to Galicia, including the widow of Henry V of England, William of Aquitaine, Louis VII of France, and eventually St. Dominic of Guzman, St. Francis of Assisi, and St. Isabella of Portugal. In the Middle Ages, a pilgrimage to Santiago de Compostela was often imposed as a penance by clergy or as a punishment by civil judges. Santiago de Compostela ranked with Rome and Jerusalem as one of the major pilgrimage sites of Christendom, and crusaders to the Holy Land often visited Compostela first. Although many other shrines sprang up across Europe, all pilgrimage roads led ultimately to Compostela.

Initially established to protect travelers on the road to Compostela, the military order of the Knights of Santiago was approved by the pope in 1195 (Plate 55). Hospitals and inns to accommodate the pilgrims sprang up along the Road to Compostela, and a whole literature developed with guidebooks for pilgrims in many languages including Spanish, English, French, Latin, German, and Italian. A booming souvenir business also evolved with scallop shell badges made of embroidered cloth, silver, jet, or lead being the most popular item (Plates 59, 64). How the shell became associated with St. James is unclear, but it may be related to a legend that a bridegroom's runaway horse took him into the sea where he was raised up by scallop shells after invoking St. James. Pilgrims also ate shellfish when they visited Compostela and used scallop shells as drinking and eating utensils. Regardless of the exact connection, pilgrims to Santiago wore cockleshells on their hats and cloaks as a badge of their journey (Plates 4, 5), and imagery of St. James from the period often presents him so dressed.

In the second half of the eleventh century, a number of factors coalesced to create a new prosperity and vitality in Europe. At last Christianity had been accepted throughout Europe creating a new religious enthusiasm that was reflected in increased pilgrimage traffic to sacred sites and culminated in the First Crusade to the Holy Land in 1095. The reopening of Mediterranean trade routes, the revival of commerce and manufacturing, and the resulting growth of city life, all contributed to the increased prosperity and a growing middle class.

The new prosperity inspired an astonishing increase in building activity and a sudden burst of architectural innovation. As a French monk described it, "It was as if the whole earth, having cast off the old by shaking itself, were clothing itself everywhere in the white mantle of churches."[3] Spontaneously and independently, a new style of architecture evolved all over Europe. Churches in the new style, now known as Romanesque or "Roman-looking," sprang up along the pilgrimage routes. They were much larger and more richly decorated than any of their predecessors (Plate 31). Instead of wooden roofs, their naves were now vaulted (Plate 3), and the exteriors were articulated with architectural ornament and figurative sculpture. They were built in the form of a complex Latin cross designed to accommodate large crowds of pilgrims. Flanking side aisles continued around the apse to create an ambulatory for crowd flow, and small chapels radiated off the ambulatory (Plate 54). The tall proportions soared to heights never before seen in architecture. Elements borrowed from Roman buildings enlivened the interior walls but were attenuated beyond reality to accent the height and seemed to reach toward the heavens.

The cathedral of Santiago de Compostela, begun in 1075, was no exception. Nine chapels in the ambulatory and transepts were consecrated in 1103, and it was finally completed in 1112. A masterpiece of Romanesque architecture, it was similar to St. Sernin in Toulouse with three naves and a wide transept, but Santiago had nine towers, very long transepts, a triforium gallery for light that circled the entire building, and six carved stone portals. Although it was extensively altered in later periods, the great core of the Romanesque structure is still dominant underneath an icing of Renaissance and Baroque decoration (Plates 60–62).

The development of Romanesque architecture instigated a revival of monumental stone sculpture. Free-standing and large-scale sculpture had all but disappeared after the fall of the Roman Empire in the fifth century. The only continuous sculpture tradition for five centuries had been miniatures or very low relief carving. The sudden revival of large stone sculpture between 1050 and 1100 reflects the growth of religious fervor among the lay population in the decades preceding the First Crusade. Exactly when and where the revival began is uncertain, but art historians agree that the cradle of its rebirth was probably in southwestern France or northern Spain along the pilgrimage route to Santiago de Compostela. Suddenly elaborate large-scale stone figures carved in deep relief populated the exteriors and interiors of the great Romanesque churches.

Like giant bibles in stone, the churches told the stories of the Old and New Testaments visually, but in silence. In painted stone, illiterate pilgrims could see miracles, heaven, and hell (Plate 14). Human and animal forms appeared to have been draped across architectural elements such as arches, columns, and pillars (Plates 7, 53). The sculptors looked at the great Roman statues still extant all over southern Europe, turned the pagan gods and heroes into saints and prophets, and placed them on the facades and walls of churches. But the figures were much more animated than most Roman statues and were now imbued with medieval intensity inherited from manuscript illumination, metalwork, and other miniature arts of the period (Plates 36, 61).

The Mission of the Apostles and scenes from the Apocalypse, such as the Last Judgment or Christ in Glory, had special meaning in the age of pilgrimage and crusades since they proclaimed the duty of every Christian to spread the Gospel to all corners of the earth before the end of the world. They also served to remind individuals of their final pilgrimage at death. As a result, they were popular subjects in the art of the period, often appearing in the tympanum above the entrance to remind pilgrims of the real reason for their journey as they prepared to enter the church (Plate 14). Particularly vivid depictions can be seen in the great Romanesque churches of Vézelay, Autun, and Moissac in southern France.

In the first half of the twelfth century, the three main entrances to the cathedral of Santiago de Compostela were the main west facade and the north and south transept entrances. These exhibited detailed carvings of Christ in Glory, the Creation and Incarnation, and the Manifestation of Christ to the World. The west facade entryway was redone between 1168 and 1183 by the Master Mateo (Plate 61). Retaining the same iconography as the earlier tympanum, the Portal of Glory represents Christ in Glory or the Transfiguration, one of the events witnessed by James, John, and Peter. Christ appears enthroned in glory and surrounded by the celestial court and angels bearing the Instruments of the Passion. On either side, humans are escorted to heaven by angels or dragged into hell by demons. Full-figure sculptures of the apostles and the prophets grace the jambs supporting the tympanum symbolizing their roles in the foundation of the Church. St. James appears on the central pillar supporting the tympanum, directly beneath Christ in Glory. As such he occupies a position second only to Christ since he was the first apostle to be martyred for Christianity. He carries his pilgrim staff and scroll, which formerly bore the inscription "Misit me Dominus" (The Lord sent me). He is seated upon the backs of lions and wears a halo of gilded copper and gems.

Miracles attributed to St. James continued to occur, sometimes on the pilgrimage route, as in the Miracle of the Fowls. Legend has it that a German couple were traveling to Compostela with their son. When they stopped over at an inn in Torlosa, the comely daughter of the innkeeper became enamored of the handsome youth, but he resisted her allurements. Angered by his rejection, the daughter hid her father's silver drinking cup in the young man's knapsack. The innkeeper discovered the loss shortly after the pilgrims' departure the following day, pursued them, and, discovering the cup in the youth's possession, accused him before a judge. The youth was found guilty and sentenced to be hanged.

After the hanging, the grieving parents continued on to Santiago de Compostela where they prayed to St. James. Thirty-six days later, on their return journey, they arrived in Torlosa to find their son still hanging from the gallows. As they stood beneath him weeping, their son spoke to them saying that St. James was sustaining him. The parents went immediately to the house of the judge and announced that their son was alive. The judge, who was seated at table preparing to dine, replied that if their son lived then so did the fowls on his dinner plate. At that moment, the birds began to crow. The judge proceeded immediately to the gallows and cut down the young man, who returned to Germany with his parents. The Miracle of the Fowls is represented in art either as a series of paintings or reliefs illustrating the various stages of the story or as a single scene, usually that of the judge at table at the moment of the revival of the fowls. But the most spectacular and, ultimately, the most important of miracles associated with St. James was that of the Battle of Clavijo.

⚔

## ST. JAMES AS WARRIOR

*Don Quixote rode up to the people, and after he had saluted them, asked what they had under the cloth.*

*"Sir," answered one of the company, "they are some carved images that are to be set up at an altar we are erecting in our town."*

*. . . Don Quixote smiled, and desired the men to show him the next image which appeared to be that of the Patron of Spain on horseback, with his sword bloody, trampling down Moors, and treading over heads.*

*"Ay, this is a Knight indeed," cried Don Quixote when he saw it, "one of those that fought in the squadrons of the Savior of the World. He is called Don Sant Iago Matamoros, or Don St. James the Moor-killer, and may be reckoned one of the most valorous saints and professors of chivalry that the earth then enjoyed, and Heaven now possesses."[4]*

St. James is reported to have appeared thirty-eight times in Spain. The most spectacular and significant of these apparitions occurred at the legendary Battle of Clavijo around 844 (Plates 20, 21). King Ramiro had vowed to stop the terrible annual tribute of one hundred virgins exacted by the ruling Moors. According to legend, he collected his troops and challenged the Moorish emir Abd-al-Rahman II:

> *The King called God to witness, that came there*
> *weal or woe,*
> *Thenceforth no maiden tribute from out Castile*
> *should go.*
> *"At least I will do battle on God Our Savior's*
> *foe,*
> *And die beneath my banner before I see it so."[5]*

With these words, Ramiro charged the Moors and a fierce battle ensued. Finally, the Christians were forced to retreat. That night Ramiro was sad at heart and fell into a deep sleep. In a vision St. James appeared to him, promised to fight with him the next day and assured him of victory. The next morning he related his vision to his troops and bid them to rely on divine assistance from St. James. Inspired with courage the soldiers rushed into the fight. Suddenly in the vanguard they saw St. James, mounted on a white charger, carrying a white banner with a red cross, and slaying Moors with his sword. He led the Christians to a decisive victory and has appeared in the vanguard of many Spanish armies since.

In religious art, Santiago Matamoros (Moor-slayer) is represented dressed as either a pilgrim or as a knight in armor. In one hand he carries a sword and the red and white banner in the other. Santiago Matamoros always rides upon his white charger and tramples infidels underneath (Plates 22, 48). One of the earliest representations of Saint James as Moor-slayer or Conqueror of the Moors appears above a thirteenth-century transept window of the cathedral at Compostela. Another early example adorns the portal of the church of Santiago in Betanzos, Spain. In this image of St. James, the two great philosophies of the Middle Ages, chivalry and religion, have merged. As such, the "son of thunder" did indeed thunder for Spain against the infidel.

It was as Santiago Matamoros that he appeared many times over the next five and a half centuries to help the Spanish Christians slowly push the Moorish invaders out of Spain and earned the reputation referred to by Don Quixote. After more than seven hundred years of Moorish occupation and domination, the last caliphate was finally defeated at Granada by Ferdinand and Isabella in 1492. The discovery of America in the same year was seen by many as affirmation by God of the Spanish cause. As a result, the spirit of Christian crusade continued in the New World, and Santiago appeared to the Spaniards eleven times during the conquest of the Americas (Plates 68, 69). Ironically, he also appeared three centuries later to assist the insurgents in Mexico's independence from Spain in 1821. He also aided the Mexicans in their 1862 struggle against French occupation and appeared a last time in 1892 during a flood in Mexico.

Although St. James appears in the art of the Americas as apostle and pilgrim, notably in the altar screens of Tecali, Xochimilco, and Huejotzingo in Mexico, he is most frequently represented in the New World as the warrior-saint (Plates 71, 74–76). Popularized by book engravings and single devotional prints since the early colonial period, Santiago Matamoros is most often depicted in full-dress armor rather than pilgrim's cloak and hat (Plates 78, 79). One of the earliest images of him in Mexico occurs in 1585 as "of sculpture, on a white horse with trappings, and the saint armed."[6] Earlier images must have existed in places named for him, such as the College of Santiago Tlatelolco founded in Mexico City in 1530, and in the capital cities of Santiago in Cuba, Guatemala, Ecuador, and Chile, founded in 1514, 1524, 1534, and 1541, respectively.

In the late sixteenth and early seventeenth centuries in the New World, Santiago appeared in relief sculptures above church portals—as he had in the Middle Ages in Europe—in such places as the cathedrals of Querétaro and Mexico City, and in the Jesuit church of La Compania in Arequipa, Peru. He also graced many New World altar screens such as the one in the military chapel of Santa Fe in the northernmost province of New Mexico, in the small village of Tilantongo in Oaxaca, Mexico, and in the Compania church in Cuzco, Peru. Life-size images of Santiago—often adorned with actual clothing and horse gear—mounted on his white charger have been commonly found in churches throughout Latin America since the sixteenth century.

The iconography of Santiago Matamoros remains remarkably constant throughout the New World with variations occurring only in clothing, horse gear, and infidels (Plates 72, 73). The medieval armor is often discarded in favor of local horse gear and clothing. In northern Mexico, for instance, Santiago may be dressed as a *charro*, or local cowboy, with the corresponding horse gear. Whereas in Chile and Argentina he may appear in the distinctive *gaucho* outfit and horse apparatus.

Santiago Matamoros had become the conqueror of Indians as well as Moors. In spite of this, he was soon adopted as a favorite saint by the Indians, possibly owing to his association with the horse. Festivals in his honor are held in many villages—sometimes with sculptures of the saint carried in procession, sometimes with an honored parishioner impersonating Santiago in a ritual dance, sometimes both (Plates 77–82). Under his feet in the Americas turbaned Moors or American Indians are depicted, but when Indians appear, they are sometimes shown protected rather than defeated by Santiago. Such is the case of the larger-than-life-size sculpture in the small church of Santa Maria Chiconautla. In such images, the Indians of the New World have taken a figure intended to represent their destruction and appropriated it for themselves by turning it into a positive symbol. In religious dance and drama in the Americas, Santiago is one of the most frequent performers. In describing such reenactments, Elizabeth Wilder Weismann has said "it is a dance of light against darkness, where the Indians seem to celebrate their own destruction. Or do they instead triumph by vicarious magic? They have the horse now, they have the shining and powerful saint, too. Santiago has perhaps been conquered by the people he thought he had subdued."[7] From New Mexico to Chile, the Indians have made him their own in dance, drama, and art.

Through the centuries in art, St. James has been depicted in all of his roles from Christian history—as apostle, pilgrim, and warrior. His image is found not only all over Europe, but also from the southwestern United States to the tip of South America, as far east as the Philippines, and even in Goa off the west coast of India (Plates 70, 83). His image graces the facades of churches in great stone carvings and appears in tiny paper prints and decals. Santiago is not only represented in all traditional two- and three-dimensional art forms, but is also "portrayed" in ritual dances by people actually dressed as the great warrior-saint either seated on a real horse or wearing a sculpted wooden horse. He is the namesake of large cities, small towns, rivers, mountains, valleys, churches, ships, mines, schools, people, and even animals all over the world. Perhaps St. James, the humble fisherman from Galilee, best deserves his avocation as pilgrim for he has indeed traveled many miles.

1. Miguel de Cervantes Saavedra, *Don Quixote* (New York: Modern Library, 1930), Chapter 58, p. 831.

2. Kenneth John Conant, *The Early Architectural History of the Cathedral of Santiago de Compostela* (Cambridge, Mass.: Harvard University Press, 1926), p. 3.

3. Frederick Hartt, *Art: A History of Painting, Sculpture and Architecture* (New York: Harry N. Abrams, 1976), p. 310.

4. Cervantes, *Don Quixote*, p. 829.

5. Anna Brownell Jameson, *Sacred and Legendary Art* (London: Longman, Green and Roberts, 1863), vol. 1, p. 234.

6. Elizabeth Wilder Weismann, *Mexico in Sculpture, 1521–1821* (Cambridge, Mass.: Harvard University Press, 1950), p. 218.

7. Weismann, *Mexico in Sculpture*, p. 177. Also see Rafael Heliodoro Valle, *Santiago en America* (Mexico: Editorial Santiago, 1946).

# PLATES

1. Roncesvalles, Spain. Pilgrims crossed the Pyrenees over Ibañeta Pass (Port de Cize) where Roland is said to have died in Charlemagne's war against the Moors. They then descended to the Augustinian Abbey of Roncesvalles. This large monastery founded in the mid-twelfth century has always provided food and lodging for pilgrims.

*2. and 3.* Near Somport, Spain. Close to the top of the southern pass over the Pyrenees is the twelfth-century Romanesque church of San Adrián de Sasave. The setting is wild. The church is isolated, abandoned, and perched in a cleft in the mountains. Over the centuries, the river from the mountains above has changed course and now flows straight through the church, around the stone altar, and out the open door.

4. The three essential pieces of equipment for modern pilgrims:
a backpack, good walking shoes, and a hat.

5. Belgian pilgrim on his way to Compostela.

6. Canfranc, Spain. Modern pilgrims can follow traces of the ancient Camino as they cross this medieval bridge in the Pyrenees and descend into Jaca.

*7. and 8.* San Juan de la Peña, Spain. This monastery, begun as a primitive hermitage in the
eighth century, is half embedded in an overhanging cliff face. The elegantly carved
Romanesque capitals on the cloister columns depict human history from
the creation to the coming of the Evangelists.

9. Jaca, Spain. This cosmopolitan town has an ancient history. It was a stronghold for the Romans, the last town to yield to the Moorish advances in 715, and one of the first to rise in support of the Christian reconquerors. It has a fine Romanesque cathedral whose builders went on to decorate other churches along the pilgrim route. The citadel shown in this photograph is a mammoth pentagonal fortress built during the sixteenth-century reign of Phillip II.

10. Pilgrim bridge, now fallen, over a deep canyon called the Foz de Lumbier.

11. Tiermas, Spain. The *Codex Calixtinus* mentions this town "where there are royal baths where the waters are perpetually hot." Today the baths are submerged beneath the Yesa Reservoir.

*12.* Eunate cloister floor.

*13.* Eunate, Spain. This octagonal Romanesque church of uncertain origin seems out of
place in the middle of a wheat field.

*14.* Romanesque carving of the Last Judgment in the tympanum over the entrance door to
the twelfth-century church of Santa María de Rocamador. Santiago appears as
one of the twelve apostles.

15. Pilgrim-scratched cross outside the door to the church of Santa María la Blanca in Villacázar de Sirga.

*16.* Puente la Reina, Spain. Modern pilgrims, like their medieval counterparts, walk over this venerable six-arched bridge that crosses the Arga River. It is here in the town of Puente la Reina that the two routes crossing the Pyrenees at Roncesvalles and Somport meet for the remaining Road to Santiago.

*17*. Cirauqui, Spain. Marker for the Road to Santiago.

*18*. Torres del Rio, Spain.

*19.* Near Villafranca Montes de Oca, Spain. Ruins of the Abbey of San Felices, part of the ninth-century monastery of San Felix de Oca.

*20. and 21.* Clavijo, Spain. According to legend, Santiago, mounted on a white horse,
appeared here in 844 to help the Christians in their battle against the Moors. A Mozarabic
castle perched high on a rocky outcropping still commands a spectacular view
of the battle plain below.

22. Sixteenth-century Santiago sculpture from the Museo del Camino at Astorga. The stone figure, wearing pilgrim clothes, is on horseback and carries a banner (and probably also carried a sword at one time). It thus combines elements of Santiago both as pilgrim and as Moor-slayer.

23. Villafranca Montes de Oca, Spain. This French pilgrim walked the Camino from Arles, France, traveling about twenty miles a day. Montes de Oca was once a fearful area covered with dense forests that were home to robbers and wild beasts that preyed on pilgrims.

*24. and 25.* San Millán de la Cogolla (Suso Monastery), Spain. In this Mozarabic church is the carved alabaster tomb of San Millán, a sixth-century hermit shepherd whose resting place became a local pilgrimage site during the Muslim occupation. The monastery was hollowed out from the rock in the eleventh century.

*26. and 27.* San Millán de la Cogolla (Suso Monastery), Spain. Leprous, lame, and blind
pilgrims visited the monastery to recover their health. Beneath the floor of the monastery
are burials of monks and pilgrims who died near here and wished
to be buried in sacred ground.

*28.* Convent of St. Anthony, near Hontanas, Spain. The monastery was founded in 1146 and offered food and care to pilgrims; most of the remaining structure dates from the fourteenth century. It is a startling apparition to modern pilgrims since the Camino passes directly under one of the arches of the great ruined walls.

29. Castrojeriz, Spain. The town is built on the side of a hill topped with the ruins of an ancient castle and was the site of battles between Moors and Christians. The land is parched and spare of vegetation. From the Middle Ages to the present time the town has offered shelter to pilgrims.

*30. Belorado, Spain*

*31. Frómista, Spain. A Belgian pilgrim traveling by bicycle breakfasts outside the Church of St. Martin, one of the most beautiful and perfect masterpieces of Romanesque architecture.*

32. Hornillos del Camino, Spain. The main street of town is the ancient Camino or Road to Santiago.

33. Carrión de los Condes, Spain. Poster for an international conference on the pilgrim route. The *Codex Calixtinus* mentions Carrión as "an accommodating and excellent town, rich in bread and wine and meat and all growing things."

34. Sahagún, Spain. Part of the ruins of the Franciscan convent La Peregrina. The town, extremely powerful in the eleventh century with a great abbey, is mentioned in the *Codex Calixtinus* as a "city abounding in all good things, where there is a meadow in which the shining lances of victorious warriors, planted there for the glory of God, are said to have once put forth leaves."

35. Mansilla de las Mulas, Spain. In the Middle Ages, this town was heavily fortified with great walls and towers, several remnants of which remain today.

36. León, Spain. Stone carvings in the cloister of the San Marcos Monastery, principal
dwelling and showpiece for the Knights of Santiago since its founding in 1168. The dagger
cross of the order appears on one of the blocks of stone. Today the San Marcos
is a luxury hotel, too expensive for most pilgrims.

37. León, Spain. A stonecarver working on restoration of the Gothic cathedral of León, known for the jewel-like beauty of its spectacular stained-glass windows.

*38*. Foncebadón, Spain. After leaving the plains of Castile and León, the pilgrim begins to climb into the León Mountains, an isolated area known as the Maragatería. Many of the villages have been abandoned; Foncebadón is still home to one family of sheepherders and a pack of unfriendly dogs.

39. Mount Irago, Spain. Tradition has it that when a pilgrim arrives at this Cruz de Ferro (Iron Cross) at the top of Mount Irago, he throws a stone on the mound below the cross.

*40. and 41.* El Acebo, Spain. In this tiny village, the houses have slate roofs and exterior staircases with balconies that hang over the road.

*42. and 43.* Ponferrada, Spain. The castle of the Knights of the Templars has been abandoned for centuries, yet details such as this key-shaped window remain to tantalize the modern pilgrim curious about the practices of this secretive medieval order.

*44*. Ponferrada, Spain. Even in ruins the castle of the Knights of the Templars dominates the industrial skyline of Ponferrada.

45. Peñalba de Santiago, Spain. High in the mountains in the Valley of Silence is the primitive village of Peñalba de Santiago. The stone houses were once monks' quarters surrounding the Mozarabic church. Today the few villagers raise chickens, bees, and a few simple crops in much the same way that their predecessors did a thousand years ago. Santiago is the town's patron saint.

46. Villafranca del Bierzo, Spain. Pilgrims arrived at the Church of St. James, a Romanesque twelfth-century church with an ornamented door called the Puerta del Perdón. Those who could go no further because of injury or illness could receive in this church all of the spiritual benefits of the complete pilgrimage to Compostela.

47. Villafranca del Bierzo, Spain. Restoration work in the Colegiata of St. Mary.

*48. and 49.* Villafranca del Bierzo, Spain. Eighteenth-century carvings on the doors of the
Church of St. James show Santiago as Moor-slayer and as pilgrim.

*50.* Herrerías, Spain. At one time this small town at the base of the Cebreiro Mountains
was known for its iron foundries. From here the pilgrim begins the most
difficult climb of the journey.

*51.* La Faba, Spain. As the pilgrim trudges slowly upward, the vegetation thins, trees disappear. Rain and fog are common in summer, snow and strong wind in the winter.

52. Cebreiro, Spain. At the top of the pass entering Galicia is the small fog-shrouded town of Cebreiro with its *pallozas* or huts of stone with thatched roofs. Every pilgrim from the Middle Ages to the present mentions his visit here and the fine hospitality provided.

53. This English pilgrim raised money for multiple sclerosis research by riding
an antique bicycle to Compostela.

54. Portomarín, Spain. This town, an ancient site mentioned in the *Codex*, was threatened
by the construction of a modern reservoir. Carefully, the villagers numbered every stone of
their lovely thirteenth-century Romanesque church and moved it to higher ground and
then built a new town around it. Fragments of the twelfth-century bridge over the
Mino River as well as some of the original buildings can still be seen when the
reservoir level falls exceptionally low.

55. Vilar de Donas, Spain. During the Middle Ages, the Knights of Santiago of Galicia were buried in this Romanesque church. Fourteenth-century murals are still visible on the walls surrounding the altar.

56. San Xulián do Camino, Spain. Galicia is the poorest and least developed area of Spain. Although highways and services are improving steadily, many families still herd a few cows and farm tiny plots of land enclosed by stone fences.

57. Leboreiro, Spain. The building to the right is an ancient pilgrim hospital and is marked by the coat of arms of the Ulloa family who founded it in the Middle Ages.

58. Spanish pilgrims near the end of their journey to Compostela.

59. Santiago de Compostela. Ever since the Middle Ages, relic shops have surrounded the cathedral and provided souvenirs for pilgrims and tourists. Most famous is the area called the Azabachería, selling jewelry of black jet.

60. Santiago de Compostela. Detail of the cathedral showing both the scallop shell and dagger cross symbols.

61. Santiago de Compostela. The cathedral of this lovely city is one of the great masterpieces of Romanesque architecture. In the Middle Ages its interior was a babble of foreign tongues, and incense was burned constantly to mask the scent of arriving pilgrims. The original facade, the elaborately carved Pórtico de la Gloria, has been beautifully preserved under a Baroque shell. Every pilgrim who enters the cathedral fits his fingers into the well-worn finger holes on this Tree of Life pillar, part of the original entry door.

62. Santiago de Compostela. This is the view from the balcony of the cathedral looking down on the grand Plaza de Obradoiro. In this Celtic city rain is common, and weeds grow from the walls. The building opposite is the Palacio de Rajoy with a statue of Santiago Matamoros on top. On July 24, the night before the Feast Day of Santiago, a crowd packs the square for a spectacular display of fireworks in honor of Spain's patron saint.

63. Chimayó, New Mexico. Outdoor services at the santuario or church at Chimayó in rural northern New Mexico. For nearly two hundred years, this small church has been a pilgrimage site. A fine statue of Santiago is placed to the right of the altar inside the church to encourage his protective spirit.

64. Chimayó, New Mexico. Peregrino (Pilgrim) Cafe and relic shop near the santuario.

65. Pilgrim arriving for services on Good Friday.

66. Chimayó, New Mexico. Nambé Indian pilgrim in front of the santuario.
In precolonial times the Pueblo Indians believed the dirt in this area had healing powers.
In 1814 a chapel was built on the site and became a pilgrimage destination. In a small hole
in the floor of a tiny room off the altar in the santuario is the healing dirt that
the faithful take away to heal injuries and illness.

67. Chimayó, New Mexico. Pilgrims entering the santuario leave their walking sticks behind.

*68.* Acoma, New Mexico. Acoma pueblo is perched high on a rocky mesa. It still appears
much as it would have to the Spanish in 1599 when they stormed the mesa and captured it
with the supernatural aid of Santiago after four days of furious fighting.

69. Ancient Indian hand and foot holds up the nearly impregnable mesa where Santiago made the most celebrated of his United States appearances.

70. Santa Fe, New Mexico. Woodcarver Luis Tapia with his Santiago made from cottonwood. For him Santiago is a "defender" of the Catholic faith.

71. An early nineteenth-century painting of Santiago on elk or buffalo hide by New
Mexican painter Molleno. It is now in a museum collection* but probably originally hung in
a rural church. Santiago was an important saint for early Hispanic settlers
who were constantly under fear of Indian attack.
*(Gift of the Historical Society of New Mexico to the Museum of New Mexico, Museum of
International Folk Art, Santa Fe)

72. *and* 73. Contemporary New Mexican Santiagos, two small retablos carved and painted on wood by Lino Roybal (left) and Richard H. Montoya (right). The clothes are more typical of a colonial New Mexican farmer than of a great warrior.

74. Santiagos from Alto Peru. A nineteenth-century palm-size soapstone carving called a *chacra piedra* or stone of the planted field. In this rural area Santiago has become a protector of the livestock. The carving was buried in the field as an amulet to protect the herd against disease and attack.

75. This elegant Santiago with velvet vest embroidered with beads and semiprecious stones and a silk cape once held reins for his rearing horse, but any dagger or banner has been lost over the centuries. Similar Santiagos were carried in retablo boxes by missionary priests in the Andes.

76. Haitian voodoo banner. Santiago or Saint Jacque Majeur, as he is known in Haiti, is associated with Ogun, the most masculine and warlike of the voodoo gods. The figure on the banner originated as a lithograph that has been entirely covered with sequins and beads except for the head, which is laminated with plastic.

77. Espinal (Veracruz), Mexico. In several areas of Mexico a *santiaguero* dance is performed. One man dances with a small white carved horse strapped around his waist; several others represent the Moors with bright red costumes. The dance is done with machetes and is seen as protective of the Catholic faith of the village.

*78. and 79.* Loíza Aldea, Puerto Rico. Santiago is an important saint throughout the Caribbean, appearing in festivals in Cuba, the Dominican Republic, Haiti, and Puerto Rico.

*80. and 81.* Loiza Aldea, Puerto Rico. In this predominately black village near San Juan, typically Hispanic processions mix with Carnival masks. These figures with wire net masks and elaborate satin costumes decorated with ribbons and sequins represent the caballero or gentleman Santiago figure.

82. Loiza Aldea, Puerto Rico. This disguise of a brightly colored bat-like cape and coconut mask with horns is called a *vejigante*. Only men wear the masks, but the women of the village do most of the work arranging the Santiago processions and fiesta.

83. Phillipine Santiago.* Santiago enjoys special veneration in the Phillipine Islands since
he symbolizes protection against the Muslim pirates who constantly
harried the Christian Filipinos.
*(Collections of the International Folk Art Foundation at the Museum of International
Folk Art, Santa Fe)

# A PILGRIM TO
## SANTIAGO DE COMPOSTELA

## *Joan Myers*

 *C'est souvent sur les grands chemins que la verité apparait aux chercheurs, ainsi qu'aux croyants. (Often on the great roads, truth appears to seekers as well as to believers.) — Courajod*

I chase a myth, I know. I push open my shuttered window and lean out into a gentle silvery rain. Across the road a thin line of black and white sheep file slowly across the wet field, their fleece matted, their bells clanging. My inn here in Roncesvalles high in the Pyrenees is built from great blocks of stone and is old enough to have sheltered generations of pilgrims.

From my high window I can see the hospital and chapel, part of the Augustinian abbey begun in the twelfth century. Beyond them the pilgrim road twists upward toward the dark pass above. In the Middle Ages and on into the eighteenth century, pilgrims coming down over the pass were met near the gate to the monastery by a monk offering bread and shelter. There were hospitals for the sick, separate houses for men and women, baths, and excellent food. In the grey rain, the massive monastery buildings squat bleakly; quietly, solidly they shoulder the weight of centuries of pilgrim visits.

My project, my excuse for the journey ahead, is not as neat and tidy as I have intimated in conversations with family and friends before leaving the United States. I am to photograph the ancient pilgrimage route to Santiago de Compostela in northwestern Spain. Along with the pilgrimages to Jerusalem and Rome, the Camino de Santiago or the Way of St. James was one of the three most heavily traveled pilgrim routes of the Middle Ages. Yet, I, too, am a pilgrim. I feel it. I go in search of answers for which I have only hazily formulated questions. I do not understand my attraction to Santiago, so often depicted as a strikingly masculine warlike figure, who lacks a historical validity and with whom I do not even share a personal history of religious faith. Perhaps by the end, I will understand the beginning.

⚜

Over the high windy pass above my inn at Roncesvalles, pilgrims from all of Europe have entered Spain for a thousand years. It seemed an appropriate place from which to begin my own journey, and so, earlier today I drove the few miles from the monastery to the top of the pass.

For me this pass will always be haunted by the ghost of Roland, Charlemagne's valiant knight, who legend has it lost his life on this barren pass battling the infidels in the eighth century. Today, on a little hill at the highest point stands a monument to fair Roland. In the Middle Ages, this desolate spot was marked by thousands of crosses left behind by pilgrims. Here, at the first stop of their Spanish journey, they knelt on the rocky soil. From the top of the pass and facing westward toward Santiago de Compostela, they bowed their heads and prayed for a safe journey.

On my visit, the pass was swathed in a wind-whipped fog. When I got out of my car and tried to photograph, the gusts made it difficult to stand upright, much less to hold steady a view camera on a tripod. I shivered in the swirling fog and then reluctantly loaded my camera back in the car. I could barely see the great stone monument to Roland, much less photograph the mountains and French fields somewhere far below. As I carefully drove back down the road to my inn, I had to be content with the words of a twelfth-century predecessor who saw this pass on a clearer day, "For the height of the mountain is so great that it seems to reach the sky. To him who ascends it, it seems that he can touch the sky with his own hand."

✠

Weary of the rain when I return, I walk over to the monastery to meet the priest in charge of greeting pilgrims. After waiting my turn with a small group of French pilgrims, all heavily loaded with backpacks and sleeping bags, I enter a small study lined with books. The priest is an intense, handsome man in a black cassock. He greets me politely and then begins to quiz me sternly about my intentions. What is the purpose of my journey, he asks me. Is it religious, spiritual, or cultural? His questions jolt me uncomfortably. I realize that in the suddenness of my decision to take on this project and all the subsequent details connected with leaving, I mentally pushed away the question of why I was doing the journey.

At first the idea was just a lark. My chance comments about an interest in pilgrimage and a desire to return to Spain after a twenty-year absence prompted a friend to send me a copy of a modern guidebook to the pilgrimage route and to encourage me to apply for a travel grant. The grant money did not materialize, but by then I already had purchased an airline ticket. My children were newly off to college; for the first time in twenty years I was free to take on a distant project. My Spanish was decidedly rusty, and I had much to learn about medieval history and Romanesque architecture. But, I loved returning to Spain and had a glimmer of a thought that pilgrimage was an apt metaphor for my own life changes.

The priest looks at me, waiting for my answer so that he can fill in the line in his great leather book. I answer him truthfully, "For the world at large, I am doing this journey for cultural reasons—to photograph this historic route for a book. For myself, the purpose is spiritual, but I do not yet know what that means." With a small hesitation, he looks at me and then smiles gently. He closes the book and tells me I am only the third American to come over the pass by mid-June of this year. He hopes I will come to the pilgrim mass that evening.

At the monastery I buy a small round cheese of sheep's milk made by the present-day monks. Lacking a knife, I cut it with my little nail scissors. It is dry and rich and unlike any cheese I've had before, and I have it with a crisp baguette, a banana, and a handful of almonds for dinner. For the first time I allow myself to feel how far from home and how alone I am. I worry about my children. I am far away if they need me. I am anxious. I feel guilty spending this concentrated time, the first such extended period in many years, on myself and my work.

At the echoing peal of the monastery bell at 8:00 P.M., I join about fifteen departing pilgrims for a short service in the monastery church. The rain has stopped, and the stained-glass windows are backlit by the strong Spanish evening sun. Five priests preside; they wear white robes embroidered with long green fleur-de-lis crosses that match the green crosses inlaid in the stone aisle. Four angels flank the Virgin over the dramatically lit altar. Each holds a gold scallop shell, the ancient symbol of the Santiago pilgrimage. Although I am not Catholic and understand only part of the liturgy, after the communion service I join the other travelers in a line before the altar. The priest prays, first in Spanish and then in French, for our safe journey. He wishes for us that we succeed in reaching Compostela, that we return home safely through whatever perils might befall us, and that we take care of each other. I walk out into a light mist with a feeling of quiet peace, a burden lifted.

Though I do not walk or bike this journey as a true pilgrim, I will travel it at almost the same speed, about fifty kilometers a day, with numerous stops and layovers for photographing. I tote a substantial load of cameras and film. I will use a large view camera for the land and architecture images and a slightly less bulky medium-format camera for portraits. The conversation with the priest and the seriousness of the short service have focused me on the task ahead, and for the first time I feel able to put away family and household concerns for the six weeks or so that it will take me to travel the four hundred miles to Santiago de Compostela.

On my drive down the pass the next morning, I give a ride to a couple I noticed at the service the evening before. Donato is a tall, heavy-set Italian in his late twenties. His girlfriend Sally is American. They both wear large white scallop shells strung on long shoe strings around their necks. They tell me they have started their pilgrimage in Roncesvalles and will hitch part way and walk part way to Compostela. As we drive, Donato gives me a nonstop history lecture on the pilgrimage route, much as if I pushed a button for a historical diorama. When he stops for breath, I ask him why he is making the pilgrimage. He hesitates, softens a little, and tells me he is not sure, that he just needs to do it. I drive them to Pamplona, and we agree to meet in Santiago.

At Pamplona I veer southeast to photograph the second of the two branches of the Camino crossing the Pyrenees from France. Although a variety of alternate routes to Santiago have been used over the centuries, these two crossings, their joining just west of Pamplona, and the road due west to Galicia have been the primary pilgrim road for centuries.

Before leaving home, I pored over maps of northern Spain, searching for tiny towns and the country roads that connected them. My decision on exactly what route to follow was made easy by an extraordinary early promotional document known as the *Codex Calixtinus*, which provides the earliest record of the precise location of the ancient route. For nearly eight hundred years, this manuscript has defined the pilgrimage route, and by default the multitude of occasionally used branches have been known as diversions.

The *Codex Calixtinus* was written in the first half of the twelfth century when the pilgrimage had already been in progress for at least a century; it was thus as much a product as a cause of it. Several versions of the manuscript exist, one of whose beauty I later marvel at in the cathedral archives in Compostela. Its exact authorship is clouded; part of it was falsely attributed to Pope Calixtus II and another part to

"Turpin," a legendary knight under Charlemagne. Modern research has shown that the codex was written as a propaganda manual by the powerful French abbey of Cluny to promote pilgrimage to Compostela.

The codex is a lengthy document, consisting of poems, hymns, and a great antiphonal mass, tales of miracles happening to pilgrims, an account of St. James's journey, martyrdom, and burial in Spain and a pseudo-history of Charlemagne and Roland. The fifth and final book is one of the first true travel guides of the Western world.[1]

It is this guidebook for pilgrims that provides the map for my journey, as well as for thousands of others through centuries past. Its French author is as ethnocentric as any nineteenth-century explorer in the wilds of the Amazon. He does not hesitate to excoriate many of the Spaniards he meets along the way. The people from the province of Narvarra, for instance, are "full of malice, swarthy in colour, ill-favoured of face, misshapen, perverse, perfidious, empty of faith and corrupt, libidinous, drunken, experienced in all violence, ferocious and wild, dishonest and reprobate, impious and harsh, cruel and contentious. . . ."[2] In addition to his frank observations on Spanish living habits and sexual proclivities, the author details stops along the journey, rivers from which one should not drink, relics that should not be missed, and the quality of the local food. Even today it makes for fine reading, and I adopted the codex route for my own.

✠

*It is good to collect things, but it is better to go on walks.*—Anatole France

I spend several days rambling about and photographing the southern pass over the Pyrenees and several sites near Jaca. The pass here is light and airy with large flocks of sheep grazing quietly in pale green meadows covered with wildflowers; it feels very different from the dark foreboding crossing at Roncesvalles.

For the first time since my arrival, I am truly enjoying photographing. I have begun to feel at ease with the unfamiliar Spanish hours for meals, the constant curious glances of passersby, and the solitude of my journey. I am still apprehensive when I wake in the morning and hear only the unrelenting sound of spoken Spanish, but I begin to trust that I can make myself understood. I am back in an old and comfortable routine of photographing; I set up the view camera, disappear under the dark cloth, slip in a holder, and snap the shutter.

Jaca, at the bottom of the pass, is a fine base for exploring the area; it is a delightful, cultured city with open-air cafes, delicious pastries, and a fragrantly landscaped park enjoyed by all in the late afternoon paseo. The cathedral, though heavily altered, shows many of the decorative attributes that reappear in other Romanesque structures along the road to Compostela. I go out every day, photograph during the morning and early afternoon, stop for a great Spanish mid-afternoon lunch, and then explore and write or read in the late afternoon and evening.

After a week I once again turn westward to rejoin the route coming down from the pass at Roncesvalles. My first stop is Tiermas, a small town listed as a stopping place in the codex but not shown on any of my modern maps. Since almost all the towns in the codex still exist (and surprisingly few new towns have sprung up in the eight centuries since), I am curious what has happened to Tiermas. Once I am nearby, the owner of a roadside cafe provides the melancholy explanation. Tiermas was famed for its hot baths from medieval times up to the mid-twentieth century. However, its baths and agricultural land, located on a plain below the town, were flooded by the recent construction of the Yesa reservoir. Without any source of livelihood, the old town high on a hill above was abandoned. It can still be seen, he tells me, from the road below.

Not far from the cafe I begin to drive along the banks of the reservoir. Speedboaters buzz back and forth across the water. Throngs of Spanish families picnic in small roadside pullouts. I glance up from the heavy traffic clogging the highway and see a town perched on a hill far above me, floating above the tumult below. I watch for a road up and finally find an unmarked turn-off. The dirt road to the top of the hill is rough for my tiny rental Ford, but once I start there is no turning back. I do my best to miss most of the ruts and boulders and to stay away from the precipitous drop on one side. I grit my teeth and then finally breathe a sigh of relief when I reach a turn-around at the top and can park the car.

Tiermas appears to have been abandoned for some time. The vegetation has grown up exuberantly around and through the crumbling buildings. Roofs have fallen in on what were grand stone homes with fine iron work and carved wood trim. Trees and wildflowers grow in what were living rooms and kitchens. Even the roof on the church has collapsed, and the bell tower is leaning precariously. The old streets, winding and curious, are nearly impassable. Waist-high weeds shoot a nasty quill-like burr into my socks and pants as I push my way through them. A strangely Lovecraftian sensation assails me. I have found a world from a previous age, left undisturbed for centuries, sleeping with all its secrets intact.

I set up my view camera and photograph for over an hour. I see no one; I hear no one. There are no clouds, and the Spanish sun is merciless. Who lived here? What happened to them? For centuries families lived in this fine walled town with its famous baths and its rich agricultural land. How did they feel about the giant reservoir that submerged their land and their history?

Then, rounding a corner I suddenly hear a dog bark and see a very old man all in black with a black beret. He has a long broom-like brush and ignores my arrival entirely as he cleans an old cement water basin. When I wish him a good day, he answers me shortly and gruffly.

"Do you live alone here," I ask?

"No, no, there are others," he says with vehemence, suggesting there would be more to find my trespass disagreeable. I follow the point of his finger and see several houses in slightly better repair than most. He rests for a moment on the handle of his broom, and then, unable to restrain his curiosity, he asks, "Where are you from?"

When I answer the United States, he gives an angry snort, turns his back on me, and resumes his work. His black dog, her teats hanging low off her skinny frame, watches me hopefully and then rolls over on her side in the shade of the water tank. I am an unreal and unwelcome visitor in a strangely real place, and fleetingly I wonder if I am the fantasy in this ancient and haunted village.

*All things considered, there are only two kinds of men in the world: those that stay at home and those that do not.—Rudyard Kipling*

A few hours later, I reach Puente la Reina, the joining point of the two passes over the Pyrenees. Out of the midday heat at last, I sit over a fine meal at the Mesón del Peregrino. I savor the roasted red peppers and lamb and ponder the attraction of pilgrimage to the human psyche.

We have ever loved to wander over the face of the earth, to explore unknown countries, and to see strange places. Since Adam and Eve ate the forbidden apple and were forced to leave the Garden of Eden, we have been travelers. Not surprisingly, Santiago de Compostela with its proximity to Cape Finisterre (the end of the known Western world in the Middle Ages) and its isolation in a Celtic, pre-Christian landscape of misty green hills and old gods has long held a special appeal.

Certainly the journey is a powerful metaphor for spiritual yearnings. Today, some two million people annually travel to Mecca, some four million go to Lourdes, and many more travel to sites on the Ganges. Pilgrimage may be one of the most universal of human ritual experiences. For thousands of years men and women have left the comforts of family, home, and friends for the uncertainties and hardships of a lengthy journey to a sacred site. Pilgrim roads have crossed the borders of provinces and empires. The purpose has been to go forth, to visit a distant holy place recognized by all.[3] An early Sanskrit text promotes the spiritual truth that all people are finally travelers and pilgrims on earth: "Living in the society of men, the best man becomes a sinner . . . therefore, wander."[4]

Although the Bible does not mention pilgrimage specifically, examples abound of "going forth"—Abraham from the land of his fathers, Adam and Eve from the Garden, Jacob from home, the Israelites from Egypt, and Jesus to the desert. Saint Augustine, not an enthusiastic traveler himself, provides a fine rationale for it when he speaks of the "violence of habit," that man must break clear of old patterns and ways of seeing the world if he is to enter a new, deeper level of existence. Anthropologist Victor Turner has put it well: "If mysticism is an interior pilgrimage, pilgrimage is an externalized mysticism."[5]

In the Middle Ages, in a rural society with few economic opportunities, the only liberation from one's village and the harshness of daily life was a pilgrimage or a crusade. In addition, pilgrims enjoyed certain privileges: they did not have to pay taxes, their property was secure from confiscation, and they could not be arrested. They were above all law except the ecclesiastical.

Most pilgrimages were made in a spirit of penance. There was a universal preoccupation with salvation and the remission of sins. The torments of hell were believed real and immediate. In a rural village, small grievances over trivial issues tended to accumulate over the years. Guilt became a nagging, heavy burden, not all of which could be relieved in the parish confessional. Disease, poverty, and economic hardship were ubiquitous and were seen as punishments that man had brought on himself. They led to a spiritual insecurity which we can only imagine in our lives of relative material comfort.

Only a pilgrimage could provide relief. It was both controlled escape and a way of achieving absolution. A person from any walk of life was believed to have an immortal soul that might be saved through penance and the intercession of the saints. In an age of miracles, these saints were as real as one's own extended family, and their lives had a veracity reinforced by omnipresent paintings and sculpture. It was firmly believed (a belief strongly encouraged by the economic and political interests of the church) that a saint was most likely to intercede on one's behalf if approached through the penance of pilgrimage.

During the height of the Santiago pilgrimage from the eleventh to the fifteenth century, this small town of Puente la Reina where I sit over my fine meal was a busy trading center. As the place where the various pilgrim roads from France joined and became a single road to Compostela, it was a meeting place for merchants and pilgrims of many nationalities.

What kind of people were these pilgrims? They came from all over Europe and from all classes of society—kings and queens to common criminals. Columbus's first act on recrossing the Atlantic after his discovery of the New World was to make a pilgrimage (though not to Compostela). Knights who survived an important battle vowed to make the journey. Priests, monks, even a few popes traveled to Compostela as an expression of their faith. Merchants, artists, as well as robbers and beggars used the road as a means of making a living. A variety of petty criminals fulfilled legal sentences that required them to return to their home towns with a certificate from Compostela showing they completed the pilgrimage. Many pilgrims were simply devout villagers who sought salvation.

All of these groups had a common uniform that appears in countless paintings and sculptures. All wore a heavy cape that served as raincoat and night blanket, heavy sandals, a broad-brimmed felt hat turned up in the front and marked with a scallop shell. They carried an eight-foot staff with a gourd attached for carrying water. "And how should I know your true love?" Ophelia sings in an ancient ballad in *Hamlet*. "O, by his cockle hat and staff, and by his sandals shoone."

Women made the pilgrimage, too. A fourteenth-century manuscript notes that the unborn children of pregnant women who were members of the French society of St. Jacques were automatically made members when they were born, indicating that both women and children made the journey.[6] Since the few surviving early journals were written by men, and the art was primarily done by men, few records survive of women's travel. I wish for their journals and wonder how they dressed, what they ate, and how they fared on the lengthy and dangerous journey.

Like the medieval pilgrim, I walk the long Calle Mayor past the church, between tall homes with carved corbeled roofs and walls ornamented with the shields of noble families. When I pass through the city gate, I step directly out on a bridge that is one of the wonders of this road. It is pure, simple, solid, and as lovely as any bridge I have ever seen. It dates from the twelfth century, and though it is now superseded by a modern bridge for cars, it is still used for foot traffic. For an ancient bridge it is wide, wide enough that two carts might easily pass. The center arc is half a circle, and its reflection in the water below forms a bright full circle of light. Bridges are passages—over, from, to, and in between departure and arrival. This one with its graduated stone arches is as gracefully perfect as it was when St. Francis of Assisi supposedly crossed it in 1214 on his way to Compostela.

I have a greater respect today for real pilgrims. I have seen many with knapsack, shorts, and t-shirts. Some are lightly loaded, others heavily. All show the strain of the work in their faces. The road coming here is more rugged than I imagined and has many hills and curves. Walking is little fun today in the cold rain. As I was photographing this morning, I met an older man who, though Spanish, has lived in France since the Civil War; he walked all the way from Arles. He is doing the pilgrimage, he told me, "to gather strength." His wife died, and he has two small children to raise. Every couple of years he takes six weeks for himself and walks the pilgrimage route. Though I too am wet and tired and a little sore from the unaccustomed exertion of lugging around so much heavy camera equipment, I feel ashamed of my warm and comfortable little car.

Several days later, I am walking a small portion of the Camino from near Sahagún, one of the codex stops, to Mansilla de las Mulas, a walled city fairly close to León. I have chosen this section of the

Camino not for its exceptional beauty or architectural treasures but because the wide open plains of Castile and León are for me such prototypical Spanish countryside.

I set off early as the mid-summer sky is just beginning to lighten and travel three miles before the sun rises above the horizon. I travel lightly, carrying only water, a sandwich, and a small notebook. I leave behind all my camera gear and feel free and a little vulnerable without my usual baggage. I wear a broad-brimmed straw hat against the coming heat of the sun. The countryside ahead of me is so totally flat that I can see the curve of the earth at the horizon. As the sun slowly rises, the reddish hue of the sky blends into the red clay of the road and fields, and I imagine myself on another planet, not just in another land.

The first small town, Bercianos del Real Camino, appears as a clump of square houses made in a child's sandbox. With its red mud houses it is a mere extension of the landscape. As I approach it, I see an enormous hawk swoop down, pluck a several-foot-long snake from the side of the road, and soar off over my head. Despite the emptiness and minimalism, I like this part of the Camino. It reminds me of the spare rolling landscape and sun-baked towns of northeastern New Mexico and western Oklahoma, country that is home to me.

I walk slowly through Bercianos, smiling at two small boys playing marbles in the dirt and wishing a good morning to a man loading long tin milk containers into his small truck. By a marshy pond full of croaking frogs I meet an old woman in black leaning heavily on her cane. I ask her if this is the road to Burgo Ranero. Through a toothless, half-formed smile she says, "Hombre! I'm not sure, but I think so." She has lived here all her life, she tells me, and has never visited the next town not more than a couple miles away.

As I set off again I recall Laffi, a pilgrim on this road in 1581, and the dead body he and his companions found being devoured by two wolves near here. They put the animals to flight and notified the authorities in the next town of Burgo Ranero to bury the body.

In Reliego, I relax for some moments out of the sun in the cool shadow at the side of the church. I take off my shoes, sprawl on the ground, and eat my sandwich. This pilgrimage is felt in the feet, the back, and the head. I am thankful for my hat. I have begun to weary of the unrelenting open space, solitude, and beating sun. Not a single cloud alleviates the fierce clarity of the blue bowl overhead.

At the sound of voices and running water, I scramble to my feet. Around the corner of the church I find three pilgrims filling their water bottles from the village fountain and brushing their teeth. Paul is sixty-eight from Grenoble. He is a wiry, quick man who has obviously done a lot of walking. He is very courteous and quick to make a light comment. He tells me he is doing the pilgrimage for spiritual reasons. "Sometime in your life you must do something like this," he says. One of his companions is a young Belgian, the other a heavy-set, taciturn German. They are companions who would have never have met anywhere else but on such a journey. We chat, and I gratefully accept their invitation to join their company for the remaining walk into Mansilla.

In Mansilla we relax for several hours over a late lunch with a great local wine. We have no common language. Paul speaks French and Spanish, the Belgian speaks English, French, and German, and the German speaks English and German. We have a wonderful time, and I realize that this polyglot of languages is also part of the history of this pilgrimage. I am amused to learn that although Paul and his German companion also have no common language, they have nonetheless become fine friends and traveled together since they met in Pamplona. Their usual day consists of fifteen miles in the morning and a like amount before dark. For me, fifteen miles is more than enough for a day's outing, and I bid them farewell.

⚔

*There is in the place and in the road, a singular poetry. . . . One is, as perhaps never before, emotionally and intellectually stimulated. Chords in the memory, long unused, are set vibrating. Like a cosmic phenomenon (it) overwhelms with the sense of its force, its inevitability.—Kingsley Porter*

My journey is more than half over, and finally I find myself off the flat plains of Castile and León. For several days, I stayed in León and enjoyed the amenities of the city, the spectacular stained glass of its jewel-like cathedral, and the remarkably preserved twelfth-century frescos of San Isidoro. Then, as I drove west from León I began to see the faint outline of mountains in the distant west. An occasional hill began to break the monotony of the plains. Many of the small towns had "Del Camino" or "De Santiago" as part of their name, linking them to the centuries-old pilgrimage.

After spending a couple days in Astorga, I begin to photograph the ancient and largely deserted villages to the west in the Mountains of León, an area known as the Maragatería. All the houses in the small villages are of stone with roofs of straw, and most are either abandoned or in a state of considerable disrepair.

The town of Foncebadón has an extraordinary location high on the side of Mt. Irago with a view all the way down to Astorga. I walk slowly up the center street past a simple wood cross and discover that the town is deserted except for one family who are shearing sheep on the rocky ground outside their home. The sky is wildly lit by a dark storm that has the nervous energy of a caged lion, growling, quickly pacing back and forth. With little effort, I can imagine this town as it would have been in the Middle Ages. Both animals and people would have lived together in these small stone houses. Pilgrims would have called out as they walked up the street in their cloaks, hats, and staffs, greeting the villagers. They would have stopped to rest and have a drink of water at the wood cross before heading on up the pass.

✚

Ponferrada. What an ugly noisy town this is, yet it has an elan, a genie-spirit who takes great pleasure in life. As I write I hear a screech of tires, metal hitting metal, and then breaking glass. I cannot see the accident from my hotel window, but can only assume it is not serious since the next sound is clapping and olé's. What an indomitable spirit the Spanish have!

Again I am enjoying the small luxuries and bustle of a city after a week of photographing in the lonely mountains. Day after day of driving along narrow, ill-kept country roads, of moving to a different cheap pension in a new town each night, of setting up the view camera and tripod and loading holders has drained me. I have been feeling rootless and very far from home. I take a room in a good hotel for three nights. I treat myself to a long bubble bath and a special dinner. I watch a bullfight on the first television I have seen in a month.

By morning I have revived and cannot resist exploring an alternate route from Astorga that I suspect may have been an early alternate route of the Camino. I drive south of the city on a narrow highway that first ascends a low mustard-colored hill for a smoggy overview of the industrial jumble below, then slips down into a valley and begins to climb alongside a little river. The trees get larger, the river runs faster, and the ferns and low vegetation get wilder.

The road curves abruptly through a tiny town of sleeping dogs, blue-green pole beans, and old men and women with antique hoes and scythes. I cross a stone bridge on which the ferns grow as easily as they do along the river. A tiny waterfall makes up in simple wonder what it lacks in size. Here nymphs and elves come to play.

Then upward, upward I drive on a one-lane paved road with many blind curves, sheer drops, and every so often a partial cave-in of the road on the cliff side. Not knowing who uses this road, I honk as I go around the curves, but I meet no one. This is the Valle de Silencio, the Valley of Silence. In the Middle Ages, monks came here to live in the caves that honeycomb the mountains, vowing to speak to God alone. Human speech does seem superfluous here; the place has the richness, the rise and fall of Gregorian chant.

Several times I am tempted to turn around; I feel a little crazy to continue following this precipitous magic road. Then I glimpse small stone buildings and a moment later pull to a stop as the road abruptly ends. I am at the edge of a village, Peñalba de Santiago, that might easily have slipped out of a time capsule from the Middle Ages. The houses are all of brown stone with grey slate roofs and dark wood doors and eves. They were originally the monks' quarters for a tenth-century Mozarabic monastery and church. The church, which has been beautifully preserved, is a simple building with a double horse-shoe arch entrance. But it is the setting that is truly a vision from a dream—sharp, pale grey peaks softened by light green vegetation and topped by low clouds.

Señor Angel Rodríguez García appears with a key to let me into the church, and I marvel at its half-barreled ceilings and the fragments of the vivid Moorish frescos that once totally covered it. Santiago is the patron saint of the village, he tells me. One side chapel has a fifteenth-century statue of Santiago as pilgrim and a banner with Santiago on horseback, sword in hand, slaying Moors.

Señor Rodríguez García tells me that he was born in Peñalba and herded sheep on the mountains above the town as a boy. He has been caretaker of the church for twenty-two years and is proud to have de-voted almost a third of his life to its protection. He tells me that indeed a branch of the Camino came from Astorga over the mountains above to Peñalba and then down to Ponferrada—for those pilgrims who wished to visit the monastery and church here. With the spectacular ruggedness of these cliffs, what a journey that must have been!

Señor Rodríguez García, true to his mission, keeps a sharp eye on me as I climb up the old stone stairs outside the church for a view of the roofs and mountains. I admire the view, which is one of the most breathtakingly beautiful I have ever seen, and I call down to him saying I wouldn't mind living here. In all seriousness, he quickly re-sponds that he has a house he can sell me, a fine house. "I'll give you the key to the door today. . . ." Quickly I am brought back to reality. The few people who live here are very poor, unable to fix up their houses with modern amenities or to move, much less to conceive of a trip to the United States. They work very hard in their small steep fields to grow enough to eat. A woman offers me fresh cherries from a basket so heavy she can hardly carry it. Another very old woman walks through the streets with a thin stick herding her five chickens. Do they lay for you, I ask? Sometimes, she says.

As I walk out to my car I stop to say goodbye to five women relaxing in the sun against a wall. We talk and watch the bee hives on the hill above. One woman hands me a bouquet of lusciously fragrant red trumpet-shaped flowers. For your Camino, she says.

✠

*There's no discouragement*
*Shall make him once relent*
*His first avowed intent*
*To be a pilgrim.* —*John Bunyon*

Again I am walking a short segment of the ancient road, this time to get a walker's flavor of Spain's northwest province of Galicia. Setting off in the cool early morning from Palos do Rei, I can sniff the end of my journey; Santiago de Compostela is only sixty-three kilometers away, and though I will not reach it today, I set off with its scent in my nostrils.

What a different world Galicia is from the heat and light-clogged plains of Castile and León. Several nights ago in the mountain top town of Cebreiro, high on the pass entering Galicia, it rained all night—something inconceivable in the dusty summer dryness of the central plains. This morning I set off in a thin mist rising from the trees and road. Walking along, I can imagine myself in Ireland with all the bright green fields and stone fences. By the time I reach San Xulián do Camino, the sun has banished the mist and is warming my chill. A man cutting the hair of a small child in front of one of the houses smiles as I wave. I begin to see *horreos*, the rectangular slatted cabinets on stone feet that are used here to store corn and wheat so the rats cannot get at the grain. I walk behind a man and woman with long sticks pushing two great cows ahead of them.

Just beyond Leboreiro I stop for coffee and meet a Catalán pilgrim. Pera is a grey-haired lithe man who teaches Catalán in Barcelona and writes poetry in his spare time. He has pulled a leg tendon and is waiting for several friends with a car to drive him to Compostela.

He is discouraged to be so close and be unable to finish the journey on foot.

We share memories and argue good-naturedly about the relative merits of towns passed. He tells me that the cemeteries around the churches here in Galicia are unique to this area. All the graves are crowded within the walls of the church yard, many above ground. One cannot enter the church without walking over graves! I ask him why he is walking the Camino. He replies that he was bored with year after year the same vacation on the beach with his wife and children. He jokingly mentioned the pilgrimage to a friend over a glass of wine one evening, and his friend took him up on it. We part and agree to meet as a group in Compostela for the festivities of July 25.

As the end of my own journey approaches, I begin to think of the work I have done. What are these several hundred film negatives I have taken of a medieval pilgrimage route across northern Spain? They have little to do with my own experience as pilgrim. The images of architecture, landscape, and iconography show only the exterior signposts of what has been an inner journey. Few photos show the symbols most real to my own journey—the heat and brilliance of the Spanish sun, the sagging beds and luke-cold drippy showers, the octopus boiled over a wood fire at a country fair, the long conversations with pilgrims and innkeepers, the pride and generosity of those who live along the Camino to the pilgrims who travel it. Even less do they speak of the exhilaration of the first weeks and the rhythm and process of the journey. I have felt myself open out like the landscape before me.

*Any man may be called a pilgrim who leaveth the place of his birth; more narrowly speaking, he is only a pilgrim who goeth towards or forwards the House of St. James.—Dante*

"Mont joie . . . je suis roi!" It is the traditional cry for the first of a band of pilgrims who, having reached the crest of the last hill, sees the spires of the cathedral in the distance. The surname King or Konig, as well as the children's game "King of the Mountain", derive from this ancient shout of triumphant arrival. I am alone as I climb the small unmarked hill littered with garbage, but I find the traditional cry still comes to my lips as I reach the top and suddenly see the four steeples of the grand cathedral of Santiago de Compostela. I thrill to the pleasure of a ritual shared by so many pilgrims of different countries and cultures. It is a moment where emotion is much stronger than the desire to photograph, and I sit down in the debris of bottle tops and paper sacks and stare out at the city beyond. How many hundreds of thousands of pilgrims have shouted their joy from this place?

Sitting amidst the debris of a modern world gone mad, I contemplate the exultation of those who have gone before me and climbed this same hill. For a thousand years, the Santiago pilgrimage has continued to attract pilgrims of different ages, cultures, and creeds. Its continued appeal for those who today walk, bike, or ride it is, I believe, a way of sharing community and spiritual goals in an era of increased fragmentation and separation.

One cannot walk a month or more without dreaming! Today, just as in the Middle Ages, we yearn for something greater than the details of everyday life. We struggle to understand our place in the universe and the reason for our existence. The old myths both enlarged humanity's sense of itself and fed the will to overcome fear of the unknown. Through them, we slowly built a network of cultures with interwoven symbols and history. The yearning for community and for spiritual answers, so profoundly human, is increasingly difficult to acknowledge, much less address, as culture becomes more complex and fragmented.

✠

*Shed of everything else*
*I still have some lice*
*I picked up on the road—*
*Crawling on my summer robes.—Basho*

Santiago de Compostela! My hotel is the Hostal Alameda, only a few blocks from the Plaza del Obraidoro and the cathedral. The owner and his wife and daughter immediately welcome me, help me unload equipment, and show me where to park my car. The city, so sleepy much of the year, is crammed with tourists and pilgrims in this week before July 25, the Feast Day of Santiago, and I am relieved not to have to drive farther.

I set off on foot down a curvy street lined with high stone buildings, climb a steep flight of steps, and suddenly find myself at the corner of one of the largest and most finely proportioned plazas in Europe. Directly across from me is the baroque facade of the cathedral with a greater-than-life-size statue of Santiago as pilgrim prominently situated. Several trucks, bright red with long ladders, are parked in the square with workmen busily stringing the fireworks across the facade for the grand display to be held the evening of July 24.

Rather than enter the cathedral via the grand front steps with the throngs of tourists, I slip around to the side. I walk through the small plaza traditionally used as a gathering place for pilgrims and enter through the side door, the Puerta de la Azabachería (named after the black jet jewelry sold in shops in the street nearby). I pause for a moment to let my eyes adjust to the dim light and to watch visitors light candles before a nearly life-size Santiago Matamoros statue.

Then I slowly walk into the central nave of the cathedral. I find tears in my eyes—relief at the end of a journey which has been both challenging and lonely, pleasure at the accumulated joy of what I have seen and experienced, and astonishment at the beauty of this structure. How can a photograph do justice to the glowing illumination of a Romanesque cathedral or to the sense of space, both soaring upward and comfortingly enclosed and human?

Nor can a photograph emotionally describe the extravagance of the Romanesque carving. Musicians, dancers, angels, and all the damned cohabit with disorderly abandon. The original entrance to the cathedral, the Pórtico de la Gloria, is now covered by the later baroque facade, perhaps fortunately, for its delicate beauty has been preserved from continued damage from the elements. Built some fifty years after the central nave and transept, it is one of the glories of twelfth-century sculpture. Like so many before me, I stand in front of the elaborately carved Tree of Life, place my fingers on the smooth, well-worn indentations in the stone, and lean down to touch my forehead to the stone head of Master Mateo chiseled below. It is a way of giving thanks and perhaps sharing a tiny bit of the wisdom of this sculptor, who so many centuries ago carved his own head here.

When I once again step out into the low sun of the Galician afternoon, I realize I have one more emotion to feel—a sadness that my journey has ended and a strange awareness that an invisible change has occurred. I set off from Roncesvalles without knowing what I was seeking or why I was retracing a thousand-year-old pilgrim road. I knew only that the journey marked a transition in my life.

Thinking back to that beginning six weeks ago, I realize it has been the trip itself, not the answers to questions that has been important for me. I have trod an ancient path, symbol of a mythic history, and it has led me to a recognition of my need for integration, community, for simple perseverance. It has been the process of the journey—the awareness of the distance yet to travel and the uncertainty of what lay ahead, the necessity for self-reliance, and the need to admit my limitations. I have a new appreciation for the simple necessities of food, a place to sleep, water to drink, and companionship. The separation from all that was familiar, the open landscape, and the sense of community have turned me inside out. It is not Santiago the aggressive slayer of infidels who has been my guide but rather Santiago as pilgrim, dressed in a simple cloak, hat, and sandals, trudging slowly across the hot, open plains, rocky passes, and misty hills of northern Spain.

## NOTES

1. The *Codex Calixtinus* will soon be available in an annotated English translation entitled *The Pilgrim's Guide to Santiago de Compostela*, edited by Paula Gerson, Annie Shaver-Crandell, M. Alison Stones (London: Harvey Miller Publishers, expected 1991). I am grateful to the authors for sharing their manuscript with me.

2. Ibid.

3. Eleanor Munro, *On Glory Roads* (New York: Thames and Hudson, 1987), pp. xi–xiv.

4. Diana L. Eck, *Banaras, City of Light* (New York: Alfred A. Konpf, 1982), p. 22.

5. Victor and Edith Turner, *Image and Pilgrimage in Christian Culture* (New York: Columbia University Press, 1978), p. 7.

6. From a conversation with Janine Warcollier, secretary of the Societé des Amis de Saint Jacque in Paris.

## FURTHER READING

An extensive bibliography exists on the pilgrimage to Santiago de Compostela. The following sources are especially helpful to the general reader: James Michener, *Iberia* (New York: Random House, 1968); Edwin Mullins, *The Pilgrimage to Santiago* (New York: Taplinger Publishing Company, 1974); A. Kingsley Porter, *Romanesque Sculpture of the Pilgrimage Roads* (New York: Hacker Art Books, 1966, 3 vols.); Walter Starkie, *The Road to Santiago* (Berkeley: University of California Press, 1965); and Brian and Marcus Tate, *The Pilgrim Route to Santiago* (Oxford: Phaidon Press Limited, 1987).

SANTIAGO
*Saint of Two Worlds*

Edited by Dana Asbury
Designed by Milenda Nan Ok Lee
Typography in Palatino
by Tseng Information Systems, Inc.
Printed by Dai Nippon Printing Company
Printed in Japan